Exploding Aspirations

Rajiv Kumar a well-known economist and author of several books, is Senior Fellow at the Centre for Policy Research (CPR), New Delhi. Earlier, he was the Secretary-General of the Federation of Indian Chambers of Commerce and Industry (FICCI). He was also Director and Chief Executive of the Indian Council for Research on International Economic Relations (ICRIER), one of India's top economic policy think tanks. Dr Kumar was a member of the National Security Advisory Board for 2006-2008. From 1987-1989, he taught at the Indian Institute of Foreign Trade (IIFT); subsequently, he worked for the Government of India from 1989 to 1995, first in the Bureau of Industrial Costs and Prices, Ministry of Industry and then as Economic Adviser in the Department of Economic Affairs Ministry of Finance. In 1995, he joined the Asian Development Bank, in Manila and assumed several positions during his 10-year term. He has a DPhil in Economics from Oxford University and a PhD from Lucknow University.

Exploding Aspirations

Unlocking India's Future

RAJIV KUMAR

ACADEMIC FOUNDATION
NEW DELHI

www.academicfoundation.com

First published in 2014
by

ACADEMIC FOUNDATION
4772-73 / 23 Bharat Ram Road, (23 Ansari Road),
Darya Ganj, New Delhi - 110 002 (India).
Phones : 23245001 / 02 / 03 / 04.
Fax : +91-11-23245005.
E-mail : books@academicfoundation.com
www.academicfoundation.com

Disclaimer:
The opinions/views/findings expressed in this book are solely those of the author and do not necessarily reflect the views of the publisher.

Cataloging in Publication Data--DK
Courtesy: D.K. Agencies (P) Ltd. <docinfo@dkagencies.com>

Kumar, Rajiv, 1951-
Exploding aspirations : unlocking India's future / Rajiv Kumar.
p. cm.
ISBN 9789332701540

1. Macroeconomics. 2. India--Economic policy--1991- 3. India--Politics and government--21st century. I. Title.

DDC 330.954 23

Typeset by Italics India, New Delhi.

Printed and bound by The Book Mint, New Delhi.
www.thebookmint.in

Contents

II
Sectoral Issues

III
Reforms and the Political Process

IV
South Asia

V
India and the Global Economy

Dedicated to my mother

Smt Sarla Prakash

who taught me the value of hard work
by her own example

Introduction

I

UPA I and II: The Missed Opportunity

India's uncertain development journey continues. "Many Futures of India", the title of the previous volume containing my columns (Academic Foundation, 2011) emphasised that despite the strong growth performance during 1999 to 2010, India faced an uncertain future and actual outcomes depended on policy choices made by the ruling dispensation. With the Indian economy having recorded an average GDP growth rate of 7.28 per cent over the 11 year period, my nervousness about the country's future was generally seen as an economist's inherent pessimism. Developments after 2010 and in the last three years of United Progressive Alliance (UPA-II's) rule have unfortunately shown that my warning was more prescient than even I could have imagined. The economy perceptibly lost its growth momentum with GDP growth rate slumping to below 5 per cent both in 2012 and 2013. Moreover, the external sector tethered on the brink of a major crisis in the second half of 2013 from which it was pulled back just in time. Private investment virtually came to a halt with Indian investors actively scouring investment opportunities abroad. A sense of despondency and despair descended on the population with successive revelations of scams and systemic corruption. As in the past, India had shown its uncanny ability to 'snatch defeat from the jaws of victory.' The country once again faced its 'many futures' as 2014 parliamentary elections drew closer.

After registering an average growth of 7.28 per cent for over 11 years, GDP growth came down sharply to less than 5 per cent in 2012-13 and 2013-14. Worse still manufacturing sector growth recorded a negative 0.2 per cent in 2013-14 and 1.1 per cent during 2012-13, declining from its peak of 14.3 per cent in 2007-08. The negative growth brought manufacturing's share even lower to 15.2 per cent of the GDP from 16 per cent in the 1990s. Exports declined by 22 per cent in 2011-12 and contracted by a negative 1.2 per cent in 2012-13 and then improved to 4 per cent in 2013-14. Services sector growth, which has been driving the overall GDP growth because of its dynamism and abnormally large share of 60 per cent in the GDP, also weakened sharply from an average of 9.35 per cent during 2003-2011 to 6.9 per cent in 2012-13 and then to 6.8 per cent in 2013-14. In July-August 2013, when the Reserve Bank of India's (RBI) irrational attempt to defend the Rupee brought chaos to the currency markets and saw the Rupee plummeting to a low of 68 to the dollar, an external sector crisis seemed imminent. With private investment virtually coming to a halt; public sector savings declining to 8.40 per cent from their peak of 17.31 per cent in 2007-08; and international credit rating agencies poised to downgrade the country's ratings, the economy, which was soaring until 2011, seemed suddenly to be in the midst of a major crisis.

There can be several explanations for this economic implosion at a time when the economy, having weathered the post-Lehman crisis, looked set for continued high growth. The least credible explanation, which was routinely put out by UPA leaders and senior government economists was that, the slowdown in India's economic growth and virtual stoppage of private investment was a result of worsening global conditions in the aftermath of the Lehman crisis. This simply does not wash and lacks all credibility. The Indian economy chalked up a growth rates of 6.72 per cent and 8.59 per cent during 2008-09 and 2009-10 respectively when the global economy was going through its worst patch with global GDP registering growth rates of 3.1 per cent and -0.7 per cent in those years following the Lehman crisis in September 2008. Even in 2010-11 and 2011-12, GDP grew at 8.91 per cent and 6.69 per cent respectively, clearly demonstrating that the Lehman crisis or its global aftermath did not affect the Indian economy in any manner. The economic slump in India took place in 2012-13 and 2013-14 when the global economic growth and world trade had begin to rise from their lowest points reached after the Lehman crisis. The US recovery, though weak, started in 2012 and the Euro area also stabilised that year. Japan's growth rebounded in 2013 with the onset of Abe-nomics and the unprecedented monetary easing by the Bank of Japan. It can, therefore, be surmised that global conditions had turned for the better when the Indian economic story turned turtle. To blame the external conditions for our poor performance was simple dishonesty aimed at hoodwinking the people in the hope that no one would dare question the wisdom of UPA's economic *pundits*. Some of us economists did raise contrarian voices but the government unfortunately was in no mood to pay any heed to them. Consequently, rather than take steps to arrest the decline, the government allowed policy making to drift with UPA's attention completely riveted on defending its government against charges of multiple and large scale corruption. This lack of policy response continued for nearly two and a half years during the run up to the parliamentary elections.

To my mind, three factors working together brought about the economic downturn which is still ongoing. First, the budget of February 2010 presented by Pranab Mukherjee (now the President of India) included measures that were widely perceived to be, anti-private investment. These included the infamous retro-active measure aimed at overcoming the Supreme Court judgement on capital gains tax liability in favour of Vodafone, the telecom multinational, and forcing it to pay up more than $ 2.4 billion in overdue tax on capital gains. The introduction of the General Anti Avoidance Rule (GAAR) law, which effectively made the ordinary tax payer guilty until he/she could prove him/herself innocent. This measure, a complete reversal of the existing and widely accepted practice of innocent until proven guilty, was seen by Indian businessmen as an extraordinary coercive measure. Transfer pricing rules and procedures were made draconian with little regards to allowing companies to at least generate normal level of profits. I saw at first hand the deterioration of investors' sentiment as their appeal for some rationalisation and relaxation of these direct tax provisions fell on deaf ears of the revenue department led by R.S. Gujral. There was an environment of near hostility towards private investors, based perhaps on the wrong belief that with the economy in full flight (GDP growth in 2009-10 was 8.6 per cent), private investors could not only afford to pay up the additional tax demands, but that the government could treat them shoddily. Having been treated shoddily, Indian investors voted with their feet by seeking investment opportunities abroad and literally junking investment plans in domestic ventures. This marked the beginning of the downturn in the investment cycle, which is still gripping the Indian economy.

The second factor responsible for pulling down investment and along with it economic growth was the strong signal from the Congress Party headquarters that for achieving their political goals both Mrs Sonia Gandhi and Mr Rahul Gandhi were keener on projecting a pro-poor and an anti-capitalist image in the remaining tenure of the UPA government. This was epitomised by Mr Rahul Gandhi's speech at Jagannathpur village in Odisha in August 2010, where he declared himself to be the *sepoy* representing the interests of the tribal people of Niyamgiri. He appeared completely unmindful of or even scornful of the losses that Vedanta would incur after having already invested more than a billion dollars in the smelting plant, that would be effectively starved of the bauxite after Mr Gandhi's cavalier intervention. The anti-private sector signal from Mr Rahul Gandhi expectedly made it open season for other UPA ministers to adopt extraordinarily belligerent and combative stance towards private investors. Amongst these, the Ministry of Environment and Forests, headed by Rahul's chief acolyte Jairam Ramesh, took the lead in cancelling licences with retrospective effect and declaring major areas as 'no-go' for private investment.

The Congress party, led by Rahul Gandhi, and bolstered by Mrs Gandhi's favourite National Advisory Council (NAC), had visibly adopted a political ideology that was almost entirely premised on articulating the voice of the excluded and showcasing Congress as the anti-private sector political formation. This 'left orientation' of the Congress has a long tradition dating back to Nehru's days and reinforced by Indira Gandhi's '*garibi hatao*' rhetoric. In the past, however, the Congress would 'signal left and turn right' without creating a policy logjam. This schizophrenic behaviour became impossible in the present day because the bureaucracy had lost its will to follow the rational policies and was only focused only on anticipating the 'leaders' preferences.' The sundry political leaders, focused on maximising private gains, also used the pro-poor stance to extract maximum gains from the private investor, thus reinforcing the anti-private sector behaviour across ministries. Rent seeking and crony capitalism became the norm and not the exception, which had been hitherto the case.

Congresses' preference for an anti-private sector stance in the UPA's second term was based on the assumption that the economy was already on auto-pilot and would churn out a GDP growth rate of 7-8 per cent in real terms year after year. This assumption also explains the lack of serious attention to any second generation reforms by the UPA government. This assumption if true would imply that in nominal terms, national income would increase by around 15 per cent annually and government revenues would rise by around 20 per cent each year. UPA thus saw great political advantage in focusing only on the distribution of these revenues to the 'excluded' and in being seen as a party that cared for the poor by creating new entitlements on a regular basis. UPA's unwavering focus on these entitlements was demonstrated by its insistence on legislating the 'right to education' the 'right to food security' and the expansion of the Mahatma Gandhi National Rural Employment Guarantee Act (MNREGA) programme plus massive increases in outlays on social sectors, which unfortunately did not produce the desired outcomes. For the bureaucracy ever eager to please the master, this implied open season for populism and curtains for hard pragmatic decisions and investor friendly policies.

This political strategy could have succeeded if, as in the past, some steps were taken to attract investment by improving the investment climate and building better physical infrastructure. However, Pranab Mukherjee's budgets, on the contrary, discouraged investment by introducing unfriendly tax policies and procedures. As a result, growth rate of private investment began to decline and the economy started showing clear signs of macroeconomic distress. This slowdown in investment and economic growth cut at the very roots of the crucial assumption about continued growth. Congress party's refusal to undertake necessary structural reforms for sustaining investment brought down the GDP growth rate and exacerbated inflationary pressures, thereby undercutting its own assumption and rendering infeasible its political strategy.

The onus of this fatal weakness to appreciate the necessity of reforms must be squarely put on the economic managers in the UPA regime. These were the most reputed and lauded trinity of the prime minister Dr Manmohan Singh, Deputy Chairman of the Planning Commission, Mr Montek Singh Ahluwalia, Finance Minister (in two separate stints) Mr P Chidambaram and the Chairman of the Prime Minister's Economic Advisory Council, Dr C Rangarajan. Others like Jairam Ramesh, Anand Sharma, Kamal Nath and Sharad Pawar were either too beholden to the Congress leadership to even make warning noises or else were busy in extra-curricular activities like cricket to spare a thought about the economy. The 'Economists Trinity' clearly failed to ring the alarm bells sufficiently loudly and persistently to compel the Congress High Command to jettison the NAC's advice and revert to the path of structural reforms, needed to sustain investment and growth. The Trinity's failure in doing so reveals either a cynical or a self-serving attitude, which led them to accept the mistaken policies of the Congress high command despite knowing clearly that these would result in economic disaster. Instead they persistently raised false hopes of a economic turnaround or continued to harp on global conditions being responsible for India's economic woes. The people expected this trinity to act honestly and resolutely to safeguard the economic performance even if this required them to put their jobs on the line. That they did not do so has been seen as a betrayal by the people.

The third factor that drove the economy to the ground was the policy paralysis that became endemic and widespread after 2011, once the corruption scams took center stage. This implied the refusal of senior bureaucracy to take decisions that posed even the slightest risk of being faulted on any count and which could bring them under the scanner of Central Vigilance Commissioner, the Central Bureau of Investigation or the judiciary through the route of public interest litigation. The right to information, passed by the UPA in its first tenure, also implied additional risks of public disclosure and consequent trial by the media for the wary officer. The trigger perhaps was the arrest of the former telecom secretary Mr Siddarth Behura, in the 2G scam for which the minister Mr A Raja was also sent to prison. With Behura's arrest and his inability to secure a bail for as long as 14 months, the bureaucracy was left feeling completely exposed and vulnerable. This resulted in widespread de-motivation and extreme conservatism in decision-making.

Moreover, the reports by the Comptroller and Accountant General (CAG) that brought to surface the high level of corruption in the allocation of natural resources like airwave spectrum and allocation of coal reserves resulted in almost completely distracting the government from policy making. People have questioned the CAG's abrogating for itself the right to conduct 'performance' rather than a 'technical' audit of departments from which the scams were unearthed. The methodology of imputing the magnitude of revenue foregone has also been challenged. Nevertheless, CAG's reports pointed to large scale and pervasive corruption and rent-seeking by the UPA ministers. Public knowledge of these scams and the subsequent mobilisation of the youth against rampant corruption and mal-practices by Anna Hazare on the platform of India Against Corruption, significantly de-legitimised the government and prevented it from taking crucial decisions. An apt example would be the delays in long pending defence orders, which threaten to compromise the country's security preparedness, because of the Minister's reluctance to take the necessary decisions.

The combined impact of these three factors was not only to bring economic growth below 5 per cent but also to trap the economy in 'slowflation' characterised by persistently high retail inflation and low growth. High inflation, sharp slowdown in employment opportunities and a pervasive sense of policy paralysis has generated a sense of despondency among the youth and the population in general.

Urgent action is needed before despondency turns to desperation and the young lose hope and unleash their anger on the 'unresponsive system.' It will be disastrous for India if its demographic dividend turns into a demographic disaster. The people feel betrayed by the UPA government. This would explain the likely worst ever electoral defeat for the Congress party and its allies. The people's hope is that the alternative dispensation that emerges after the elections will re-establish the government's credibility, restore economic growth, generate employment opportunities thereby reducing the gap between aspirations and outcomes.

II

India: A New Beginning

India needs a new beginning. It has to firmly steer out of the morass left behind by the UPA government with its scams, divided accountability, demoralised bureaucracy, illegitimatised government and a strangled economy. The necessary condition for moving ahead is that the 2014 elections do not deliver a fragmented political outcome. This looks increasingly likely. The Indian electorate, having recognised the dangers of a fractured outcome, will vote decisively to give the NDA a clear mandate. This has once again demonstrated the sagacity and deep sense of national purpose of the Indian electorate, which has not been duped by the counter-Modi campaign either at home or that unleashed by the Western media in the run up to the elections.

The new government will have to make a fresh start and be prepared to stay the course. It will have to resist populist urges that either satisfy petty political agendas or pander to middle class seemingly insatiable demands for subsidised consumption. India needs three decades of uninterrupted growth to banish the scourge of absolute poverty and achieve its development objectives. It could then emerge as the largest economy (in purchasing power terms) by 2050, when it celebrates its centenary as a Republic. This is a worthy and an eminently achievable goal. It will once again imbue our people with a sense of national purpose. Armed with such a purpose and led by an honest government, Indians will ensure the emergence of *Shreshta Bharat*.

The foundations for this new inspirational journey will have to be firmly laid by the new government within its first term after making a quick start within the first year of coming into office. The Government will have to initiate reforms that are within its executive mandate and steer clear of legislative traps and judicial delays. This will also enable the executive branch of the government, which has ceded space to other branches consistently over the past decade, to regain its legitimate space and restore the balance between the three branches of the government. Reform measures, designed to generate social consensus and put the economy back on track for rapid and inclusive growth will give the executive branch the necessary credibility and momentum to push forward with other longer term measures required to sustain India's resurgence.

Five major initiatives, that can be taken as executive action can be immediately taken by the new government without fear of being hampered by either the legislative or judicial processes. These are: First to reassure the people, especially the minorities, of even handed, non-discriminatory, transparent, norm based and effective governance. This is essential to minimise social dissonance, ensure broad base empowerment and thereby maximise inclusion. Second, to re-instate investors' confidence and give a fresh start to the investment cycle, which is necessary to propel economic growth. Third, to re-assure the senior bureaucracy and encourage it to be innovative in policy formulation and decisive in their implementation. Fourth, to move resolutely against systemic corruption and establish transparent and effective systems of governance that will eliminate rent seeking from government processes especially in the allocation of natural resources and government procurement. Fifth and finally, initiate steps to tackle inflation and ensure that the ghost of food inflation is laid to rest by taking steps for ramping up food production in the country.

Reinforcing peoples' faith in democratic institutions and eliminating fears, either articulated or left unspoken, about possible discrimination against any group of our population is the foremost task for the new government especially one led by Mr Modi. He has done well so far to state his clear preference for 'toilets before temples' and by distancing himself unambiguously from bigots like Praveen Togadia and Giriraj Singh. But this is merely the beginning. He and his cabinet colleagues will have to sustain their development agenda and show zero tolerance for bigotry and discrimination on communal and religious lines. The Modi government will have to demonstrate a heightened sensitivity to petty ground level discrimination by junior bureaucracy and police that becomes pervasive very quickly unless nipped in the bud. But we must also recognise that it is not an individual political leader or even a political formation that poses the real risk for communal and social strife breaking out in India. The greatest risk is posed by an imploding economy and mal-governance. The youth, seeking to apportion blame for their unemployment and wasted lives, will fall prey to communal and divisive forces. Therefore, the new government must necessarily focus sharply on the agenda for generating employment and development and not be distracted by any other so called priorities. The necessary condition for generating employment and achieve rapid growth is to re-start the investment cycle.

For restoring the investors' confidence, five steps can be immediately implemented. (i) Replace the existing forms prescribed under any applicable laws, rules, orders, and instructions for obtaining the required licences and clearances by one combined application form. This will release enormous entrepreneurial energies especially in the Micro, Small and Medium Enterprises (MSME) sector and give a fillip to investment. (ii) Introduce a system of common return that will dispense with the need to submit multiple returns with different frequency. This common return would replace most of the more than one hundred returns currently in use. (iii) To drastically reduce the time taken for starting and exiting a business. For starting a business, a time limit of three days should be implemented across the country. The average time taken for exiting a business, according to the World Bank's *Doing Business* survey, is at present a horrendous 10 years. This surely can be brought down to less than a year by establishing special tribunals or fast-tracking the adjudication process in labour courts. (iv) Seriously consider a shift to a system of self-certification rather than annual clearance by designated inspectors. This will greatly reduce the compliance burden, especially for MSMEs, where it is borne by the owner-entrepreneur. (v) Central government to encourage states to replicate the best practices that are already in place in other states with regards to the establishment of the single window for business applications, acquisition of income tax, and sales tax registration numbers, and obtaining 'carry on business' licences.

These five measures can be implemented by executive order. They do not require either legislative or judicial clearance. If implemented right away it will provide the strongest signal to both domestic and foreign investors that the new government means business.

It may perhaps sound paradoxical but the way forward for improving the bureaucracy's performance is to induct a higher number of professionals into senior government positions. This will bring much needed competition to the Indian Administrative Service (IAS), which currently sees itself as the sole repository of all governance and professional expertise. This will also provide the political leaders alternate viewpoints and some benchmarks to better judge the competence of their senior officers. The entry of the professionals is also necessary because the economy and the polity have now become far too complex to be managed by generalists alone, however, bright or intelligent.

There is some evidence that the IAS is suffering from loss of talent because of adverse selection with better quality students being attracted away to other professions on account of better salaries and higher job satisfaction. This needs to be reversed and for this the major recommendation of the Fifth Pay Commission to prune the bureaucracy but pay its senior members on par with their contemporaries in the private sector must be implemented as soon as possible. It is time that our senior bureaucrats' salary is restored to the levels in the immediate post independence period. As suggested by a former cabinet secretary, this could be easily achieved by paying them enough to purchase as much gold today as they could with their salaries in the early fifties. This will help to minimise rent-seeking, restore the social status of the bureaucracy and attract the country's best talent back to its fold.

Another important measure required to ensure the autonomy, independence and credibility of our senior bureaucracy is to streamline the process of post-retirement employment for the IAS and other members of the covenanted services. The present practice by which a plethora of quasi-government positions are available for retiring bureaucrats clearly compromises their judgement and decision-making at a time when they are heading important government departments.

Therefore, as a rule all retiring bureaucrats must be barred from taking another position in the government or allied agencies for at least one year. Once they become eligible after a cooling period of a year, they should be appointed only on the basis of an open selection process and in competition with professionals from the private sector. The example of New Zealand where all senior positions in the government are filled on the basis of an open selection process can be applied at least to all quasi-government jobs which today are decided on the basis of complete non-transparency and possibly widespread nepotism. This breeds insularity and clique behaviour, which cuts at the very root of performance and good governance. The new government should also consider extending the practice of a minimum fixed term for heads of department as already in practice for the cabinet and foreign secretaries, to give the incumbent sufficient time to design and implement the policies for which he/she is accountable.

Mr Modi's often stated mantra of 'maximum governance with minimum government' conveys the essence of a governance system that is geared to minimising and hopefully eliminating corruption and rent-seeking from all levels of the government. Public sector corruption is threatening to become (if not already so) systemic and all pervasive. Unfortunately, NDA's previous government under Mr Vajpayee was also not free from this serious taint. UPA's second tenure was characterised by repeated and large scale corruption scams, which have been significantly responsible for the strong anti-incumbency faced by the Congress. Therefore, the new government, especially one led by Mr Modi, will have to take the extra step in delivering on its promise of rooting out corruption from the government and public sector agencies. This will require maximising the use of e-governance across government departments. Public auction of natural resources and eliminating unnecessary regulations will also go a long way in minimising corruption. Equally importantly, the widespread incidence of petty corruption (bribes, speed money and commissions) that is currently rampant in the country can be eliminated simply by setting an example at the top and announcing and implementing a 'zero tolerance policy' for corruption. Indians have clearly demonstrated their preference for a corruption free government by having voted in

Mr Arvind Kejriwal's Aam Aadmi Party in to office in Delhi. The new government will have to respond to these expectations if it wishes to remain legitimate and credible.

Finally, but perhaps the most critical in the short term for providing much needed respite to the population suffering from chronic inflation, the government has to show its intent and resolve to tackle food inflation. To achieve this, it should not take recourse to knee-jerk administrative actions like banning exports of agro-products; passing some draconian laws against alleged hoarders and traders; or taking over the trading of specific commodities. These administrative measures are generally counterproductive. Instead the government will do well to set up an Expert Group to diagnose the actual causes for sustained food inflation and recommend suitable measures. The terms of reference for such an expert group will include a review of the impact of the Agriculture Produce Market Committee (APMC) act; the impediments in inter-state movement of agro-products; working of the Food Corporation of India (FCI); weaknesses in the logistics chain from the farm gate to the market that result in massive wastage of food products; and the working of the plethora of schemes designed for improving agriculture practices but which in practice remain only on paper. In addition, the expert group may also be asked to submit its recommendations for effectively addressing the food price hike that is expected in the second half of 2014 due to lower food production as a result of El Nino induced sub-normal monsoons this year.

Given the electorate's clear mandate, the new government has an unprecedented opportunity to make a clean break from the past decade and launch India once again on the path of rapid and sustained growth that will generate the needed employment opportunities and empower the people. India has to create 12 million jobs every year only to absorb new entrants to its workforce. It has to also find additional jobs for those who will leave agriculture and move to urban centres in search for higher incomes. India will reap its demographic dividend only if it successfully absorbs these entrants into productive employment. Inability to find productive employment for its young population, will result in a nightmare scenario in which the youth will be used as cannon fodder by competing groups of fundamentalists and extremists. That will bring the country dangerously close to a political and social implosion that could have enormous negative consequences for succeeding generations.

The new government, therefore, has a historical responsibility to save India from descending into a downward spiral which could result in its fragmentation and decline into a second rate global power. On the other hand, the new government could lead the country to emerge as the world's largest economy; be rightfully invited to the high table of global governance; and serve as an example for other emerging economies. The stakes could not be higher. This should motivate the prime minister and his cabinet colleagues to unwaveringly serve the national purpose and rise well above their own self interests and short term priorities. The people who have elected them expect nothing less.

I

Macroeconomic Issues

1

Beginning of Modi Era

THE PEOPLE HAVE delivered a staggering verdict beyond all expectations in favour of Mr Modi. This is historical and reflects the people's hope for structural change in India's development paradigm. The pan-Indian victory across rural, urban, tribal and constituencies dominated by different communities reflects the deep and widespread aspirations of the new Indian. Indians who are looking for employment and not doles; empowerment and not entitlements; growth and not mere distribution and transfers; good governance and not an executive devoid of direction and purpose. In short, *Bharat* with its exploding aspirations has come centre stage. It has pushed aside firmly and perhaps decisively Macaulay's India that took its reference from the West. Real India, that is *Bharat* can now rise anew, delve deep and wide into its vast pool of talent and resources and use it to strive to become *Shreshta Bharat*. An India which stands tall among the comity of nations on the basis of its own achievements.

This is the dream that Mr Modi has sold to the electorate and they have seized it with both hands. It is also clear that the dream of a prosperous India has been supported across communities and regions. This puts a mountain of expectation on Mr Modi's shoulders. He has asked for a vote for himself and he has got it in numbers that have left us and him speechless. And with the absolute majority for BJP on its own, he has no conceivable excuse for not delivering the dream. All BJP leaders, big and small, old and young, from urban and rural regions should now jettison any differences they may have had and put their shoulder to the task under the leadership of the man who has won them this unprecedented victory by his indefatigable hard work, single-minded focus, and an organisational capability that has left all others biting the dust. Now is the time to come together to take India forward and make it a *Samridh*, *Sashakt*, *Shrestha* and *Swabhimani Bharat* by the time we celebrate the centenary of our independence.

Mr Modi has to rise above all social divisions and emerge and establish himself as the leader of all Indians. The electorate has already recognised him as such by giving him 26 out of 26 seats in Gujarat and an unprecedented and unbelievable 70 out of 80 seats in UP. Such an emphatic verdict could not conceivably be achieved by the support of any particular community. But no society, and certainly not India with its syncretic *Ganga-Jumni tehzib* that Mr Modi talked about in his speech in Varanasi, can develop and progress if a significant proportion of people remain wary and alienated. So he will do well to reassure those who have not voted for him that he and his government will deliver fair, just and equitable governance to all Indians irrespective of political or ideological identity. And here actions speak far louder than words. Will he for example consider appointing his most trusted and capable aide to oversee the implementation of Sachar Committee report?

The people have already shown that they do not accept the diminution of the Prime Minister's office (PMO) or the arrogance of any royal family or dynasty. In Mr Modi, the Indian people have elected a leader who will ensure that the PMO re-emerges as the captain's cabin with the captain having a firm hand on the rudder. At the same time by promising to govern collectively not only with his cabinet but also with the chief ministers during his campaign, he has demonstrated a keen understanding of the scale, complexity and diversity of the Indian reality. He will therefore not succumb to the temptations of over-centralisation. He will also try to reinforce and enhance federalism with its huge advantage of finding and implementing region specific solutions. This would provide the provinces with the degrees of freedom and fiscal space necessary to make the Indian development experience a beautiful mosaic of regional paradigms.

Given his impeccable track record of the highest level of personal integrity and honesty, I am convinced that Mr Modi will resist all temptations for appointing anybody who has even the faintest taint of financial corruption, moral turpitude or unethical behaviour to the cabinet or high government positions. He will do well to adhere to his own high standards of personal integrity and select those who, in the best traditions of the Sangh, desire to serve the country and are not pursuing an agenda of personal aggrandisement or material gains. His team of selfless volunteers, who have worked tirelessly, with many having stayed away from their families for months, represent such a band of highly motivated individuals committed to India's cause. He will have to find similar set of individuals to fill key positions. At no cost can Mr Modi allow his government to be seen as another version of the UPA government full of self serving opportunists, willing to switch sides at the drop of a ballot. People's strong desire for clean and effective governance has to be respected and responded.

Mr Modi has built up a tremendous reputation for project execution and also for being open to innovative ideas. Armed with these strengths he can deliver on his promise of 'minimum government and maximum governance.' He has to keep open as many windows as possible for new and innovative ideas to reach him and to adopt a 'revolving door' policy for bringing in talent from the private sector, civil society and NRIs. The entry of such professional talent will improve governance and help implement key projects. This can be one of the key structural changes in sustaining rapid growth on the one hand and simultaneously ensuring effective delivery of public services on the other.

This is a new beginning for Indian democracy as it hopefully spells the end of dynasty, identity based and pseudo secularist parties. The onus of delivering on these hopes and exploding aspirations is on Mr Modi's broad shoulders. I wish him Godspeed. Not just India, but the world wants him to succeed because India's success means that development, democracy and diversity can all come together in a successful experiment.

2

Macroeconomic Concerns

THE RECENTLY RELEASED GDP growth data for the first quarter (Q1) of 2011-12 should raise concerns on the deteriorating macroeconomic situation in the country. GDP growth at 7.7 per cent in Q1 was the lowest since Q3 in 2009 and has declined successively in the last three quarters. Even the 7.7 per cent was achieved on the basis of a downward revision of GDP growth in Q1 of 2010-11. On the basis of unrevised data, growth in Q1 of the current fiscal would slip further to 7.2 per cent below the lower bound of 7.6 per cent forecast earlier by the Reserve Bank of India (RBI). Car sales are already in negative territory for both July and August and this is indicative of the state of the manufacturing sector. Construction activity has markedly slowed down with first quarter growth in the sector at a measly 1.2 per cent as compared to 5.7 per cent in Q1 last year. Agriculture growth at 3.9 per cent has been a pleasant surprise but this momentum can hardly be maintained given the high base. Services sector has maintained its double digit growth but with public sector expenditure under pressure and software exports likely to suffer on account of continued weakness in the US economy, it can hardly be expected to grow much faster in the next three quarters. Exports growth is perhaps the only silver lining with July seeing a record breaking 82 per cent growth, despite weaknesses in major global markets. But even the Commerce Secretary has warned that it is futile to expect exports to grow at this scorching pace. With the full impact of increased interest rates on domestic demand likely to be felt in the coming quarters, we should not expect the growth in the next three quarters to be any higher than in the first one. We may well see lower growth and aggregate GDP growth in 2011-12 coming in closer to 7 per cent rather than achieve government estimates of 8 per cent or thereabouts.

While it is true that the Indian economy in 2011 is vastly different from that in the period 1998-2002 when growth plummeted to as low as 2 per cent, it is hardly worth arguing that there is a floor at 7 per cent for GDP growth in India. This would be fallacious and dangerous. Most importantly, the longer our economic growth is below our potential growth rate of 9-10 per cent, we are losing opportunities for generating more employment, critically needed to absorb some of the 12 million new entrants to the labour force each year. By not maximising our potential and actual growth, we could get on to the dangerous path of rising social and political stress and unrest.

Other components of the macro situation are also worrying. Inflation refuses to come down despite the RBI having raised interest rates on 11 occasions in the past 18 months! Price data released on 2nd August show food prices increasing by 10.05 per cent for the period ending 20th August, with fruits and vegetable (F&V) prices leading the charge. It should be amply clear by now that raising interest rates is unlikely to have the desired impact on peoples consumption of fruits, vegetables and proteins and prices will stabilise only with a much stronger supply response. Unfortunately, the upward pressure in food prices is likely to be construed by the RBI as another signal for raising interest rates for the 12th time. This will surely weaken investment, consumer durables and construction demand and adversely affect overall GDP growth while leaving F&V prices untouched. The spectre of stagflation begins to lurk on the horizon!

On the fiscal front, things look equally bad. Fiscal deficit during April-July is already 55 per cent of the annual budget estimate as compared to only 24 per cent in the same period last year. Total public expenditure has remained at the same level (30%) as in the previous year. But it is important to note that at this level, public expenditure grew by 19 per cent during 2010-11, while it is required to grow only 3.6 per cent in the current fiscal. It is difficult to visualise sufficient cuts in public expenditure to bring down the growth to 3.6 per cent in the remaining eight months. Revenue receipts seemed to have slipped badly with April-July showing collection of only 17 per cent of the estimated annual receipts as compared to 35 per cent last year. The worst slippage has been in non-tax revenues of which disinvestment receipts account for the biggest chunk. In the four months last year, 85 per cent of the budgeted amounts had already been collected thanks primarily to the spectrum sales. In this year a mere 18 per cent have been raised in these four months and the prospects for the remaining period are not so bright given the depths that the sensex has been plumbing recently. In all likelihood, unless the government takes the axe to some of the welfare schemes and subsidies, the budget's fiscal deficit target of 4.6 per cent will be breached. According to FICCI's estimates it is more likely to be 5.2 per cent. This will put additional pressure on market interest rates by soaking up liquidity, in a situation where rates are already rising because of RBI action. This will do investment intentions no good at all and could result in a further decline in launching of new projects. In short, it is time to take serious stock of the country's macroeconomic situation and take action before growth heads to sub-7 per cent levels in the coming quarters. That should indeed be highly avoidable.

3

Steadily towards an Economic Abyss

OUR WORST FEARS have been confirmed. GDP growth continues to plummet and is now at a four year low of 4.4 per cent for the first quarter of the current financial year. This should hopefully stop all loose talk of 'plateauing of growth' and sightings of green shoots of recovery. It will also hopefully also put an end to the argument that this remarkably poor performance is entirely due to exogenous factors and not a result of mismanagement and simply lack of policy direction. I suppose the Governor of RBI knew these numbers yesterday when in his speech he tried to put RBI at a distance from and place the entire onus for this poor performance on the Government. I suppose too that we are all in a for a bout of hand wringing and passing the buck as the next quarter will only bring worse news than what we have already. How far would the Prime Minister's Economic Advisory Council be prepared to bring down GDP growth rate to fight its imaginary inflationary demons? Would the dream team continue to look for quick fixes while going along with fiscal deficit increasing measures or will it take courage to tell its UPA political masters that continued decline in growth rate will have the worst impact on the poor from which they will not be protected with either the FSB (Food Security Bill) or the LARR (Land Acquisition and Rehabilitation & Resettlement).

The scary feature of the GDP data released today is the decline in manufacturing sector growth rate and in the gross fixed capital formation. Manufacturing is actually shrinking in a country where manufactured imports from China are on the rise. Investors are simply on a strike and the negative growth represents they are voting with their feet and capital outflow against the government's policies and performance. In this situation, is it not a cognizable offense to pass the two bills, of which the FSB threatens to bust the fiscal balance and the LARR will undoubtedly make investors even more wary of considering any capacity expansion in the manufacturing sector. Is it not patently dishonest to now talk of the agriculture sector, boosted as it may well be by a good monsoon, to pull the economy out of its slump. Why do our policy makers forget that agriculture sector's share is a mere 13 per cent in our GDP.

With the RBI having wielded its liquidity contracting axe and pushing up market interest rates; the Rupee plunging to record lows in July and August; and government adding to the misery by worsening the investment climate through the passage of the two bills; we can hardly expect the second quarter (July to September) to be any better than the previous one. If anything, GDP growth in the second quarter will be even lower.

I do not see any reason to believe that growth rate will recover in the second half. With the Damocles' sword of the credit downgrade hanging over the Finance Minister, there is no scope for expansion in public expenditure. Consumer sentiment seems to be in the dumps as reflected in the slowest growth in a decade or more in private consumption expenditure, which has grown by, indicating a virtually stagnant consumption demand—the mainstay for growth. With rising interest rates, and higher land prices, consequent upon the enactment of LARR, there is hardly any chance of an upward tick in housing or consumer durable demand. With food inflation seriously eroding purchasing power, we cannot expect a rise in the demand of consumer non-durables either. With a government in office that seems not to bother at all about investors' sentiments and interest rates remaining high along with continuing payment difficulties in PPP projects, we are in for a further slowdown of investment demand as well. With each passing month we draw closer to the elections, which will encourage investors to shelve their decisions even more. On these counts, the second half will in all likelihood be even weaker than the first one. The only upside could come from rising exports, bolstered by the depreciating Rupee and the growth pick up in the US and Europe. But with iron ore exports still suffering from the ban on mining and manufactured sectors not particularly competitive, this export led boost could be weaker than expected. The other hope is that disbursements will pick up on the projects on investment recently cleared by the cabinet committee. Here again the problem is that if these are public sector projects, they will face an expenditure constraint. And in the case of private sector projects, investors will not be in a mood to increase their capital outlays in the face of high interest rates and rising political uncertainty. Therefore, GDP growth in the second half could well be even weaker than the first half. This leads me to believe that that we will be lucky to get a GDP growth of 4.5 per cent in 2013-14. And this does not account for some major shocks coming from global oil prices, or foreign institutional investors (FIIs) further deserting the Indian market or non-resident Indians (NRIs) deciding to pull out their deposits. These would expose the economy to a nasty external sector shock.

How one wishes that we had a political class with some sense of national priorities and be prepared to take tough necessary measures rather than be only and only concerned with their narrow and short term partisan interests. These will simply take us over the cliff into a situation from where there will be a lot of pain in climbing back.

4

State of Denial

THE CHAIRMAN of the Prime Minister Economic Advisory Committee (PMEAC) Dr C Rangarajan, was quoted on 24th April as saying that the current (XII) Five Year Plan could still see an average GDP growth of 8 per cent!. During the interview, given after the release of the latest *Economic Review* by the PMEAC, Dr Rangarajan expounded on a lowering of the incremental capital-output ratio (ICOR) resulting in higher growth in coming years. In simple terms, he expects higher growth by a de-bottlenecking of large projects that will bring down the ICOR. How one wishes it was as simple as this to get us back to a higher 8-9 per cent growth trajectory. Similarly, when in July 2011, at a seminar organised by Suman Berry, then head of the Ideas for Growth (IGC), I had pointed out to the then Chief Economic Advisor, Kaushik Basu, that investment was beginning to slacken dangerously, he simply pooh-poohed the warning. We know what happened thereafter. Investment tanked in India and Kaushik became the Chief Economist of the World Bank! Clearly, there are advantages to being in a state of denial.

In the first year of the Plan, i.e. 2012-13, economic growth will be no more than 5.2 per cent. In the next year (2013-14) it can at best rise to 6 per cent for the following reasons. Government expenditure will necessarily remain repressed as the Finance Minister tries to bring fiscal deficit below 4.8 per cent of the GDP as he has targeted in the budget. So any hopes of a pre-electoral splurge to boost aggregate demand, as was done in fiscal 2007-08 can surely be ruled out. The alternative is a hugely damaging credit downgrade that we can ill afford. So government demand will not provide a growth impetus. In fact, over the last quarter one has heard of increasing instances of non-clearance of large volumes of government dues resulting in a significant negative impact on cash flows and profitability of service providers and contracting companies.

From all accounts private investment demand is unlikely to strengthen as the investment climate continues to remain vitiated in major growth sectors like telecom, autos, steel, power generation, highways, etc. Despite all the talk of reforms since September, we have yet to see any real initiative that could boost investor spirits or promote investment. Moreover, there is now an apprehension of a major slowdown in the real estate or the construction sector, which has provided a strong growth stimulus in the past 10 years. So private investment demand, which is the strongest driver of growth, will remain weak this year. This is corroborated by demand for non-food commercial credit remaining weak and a rising level of non-performing assets (NPAs) in the banking sector.

There is hardly any reason to believe that private consumption demand will reverse its current weakening trend and start rising. Disposable incomes are unlikely to increase significantly in the absence of large scale government handouts and continued weakness of employment prospects. The ongoing decline in auto sales, declining demand for consumer durables and lower spend on consumption items like FMCG (fast moving consumer goods) products and fast food outlets are clear signs of continued consumer pessimism and the fact that the mood in the country is distinctly downbeat. Finally, despite the recent feeble uptick in export growth, and the fact that a lower base (exports actually declined in 2012-13!) may provide a basis of higher growth in 2013-14, net external demand is unlikely to emerge as a growth driver in the current year. A similar conclusion for a GDP growth of sub 6 per cent in 2013-14 can be reached by looking at the supply side and considering growth prospects in agriculture, industrial and services sector. Talk of 6.7 to 7.0 per cent growth in the current fiscal is just wishful thinking.

With the first two years of the Plan period achieving 5 and 6 per cent rate of growth, the economy will have to grow at more than 9 per cent annually in the remaining three years of the Twelfth Plan to achieve an overall average of 8 per cent GDP growth. Even for an average 7 per cent rate of growth over the plan period, GDP growth will have to jump to 8 per cent in 2014-15 and be sustained at that level. Given the onset of election season in full measure from October this year, and the prospects of significant political instability, it can only be as brave a man as Dr Rangarajan who can talk so confidently of the Twelfth Plan coming in with 8 per cent growth rate. Should there not be some accountability for government agencies to ensure that their forecasts and pronouncements are not completely out of whack from ground realities?

Such facile talk of higher growth rates is dangerous because it induces complacency when none is warranted. There are 1 million (repeat 10 lakh) new entrants to our labour force every month. These youngsters, who represent our much flaunted demographic dividend, need jobs. Without, productive employment, they will add to the hordes of urban lumpen class, which is now visible in all our neighbourhoods and colonies except of course in Luteyns Delhi. They are all aspiring for the good life, which they will seize by means fair or foul. In the absence of jobs, they will earn their livelihood by joining the gangs of touts, petty brokers, smugglers, real estate mafia. The luckier ones will pay hefty sums to get into the police force or other public sector jobs and then wreck havoc on the civil society as they attempt to recoup the bribe they paid to secure the prized '*sarkari naukri*'. It would be far more socially responsible for the government's economic managers to not show their state of permanent denial by constantly talking of higher growth being round the corner, They should instead talk of the huge employment challenge facing the country and the dire consequences of these young people remaining unemployed and spilling out on the streets. This fear apparently kept Deng Xiaoping awake at night and led him to initiate the Chinese economic miracle. I wonder what apart from the fear of losing their jobs keeps our economic policy makers awake at night!

5

Needed a Credible Plan for Recovery

IT IS CLEAR that we are entering a period of significant political instability. Three major state elections of Delhi, Madhya Pradesh and Rajasthan are scheduled for the latter half of the year followed by Chhattisgarh in January and the General Elections thereafter. It is widely expected that UPA will not do well in the forthcoming state elections. That will exacerbate the 'lame duck' nature of the ruling coalition in Delhi, and unfortunately take a further toll on the economy. With the GDP growth rate already down to 4.8 per cent in the last quarter of 2012-13, we need decisive action to bring back investment and improve the business climate. Instead the political instability and policy paralysis will take the economic growth further downwards and one shudders to think where it may all end.

The seriousness of the present economic situation and the immediate negative prospects came home starkly and with somewhat of a rude shock recently in Dubai as one spent an evening together with a few young Indian business persons. They have virtually given up on India and are shifting operations abroad and working out of Dubai rather than be "harassed and be hamstrung" in Mumbai or Delhi. Their bitter complaint is that to the extent there is any response from the mandarins and political leaders it is always in favour of the big boys of the Indian industry and the case of the smaller but rapidly growing entrepreneurs goes completely unheard. They are left to the mercy of the petty bureaucrat (the inspector and the tax collector) who do not have any other objective but to maximise their own rental incomes and secure an even more lucrative job after their current tenure is over. There are now hundreds if not thousands of relatively young Indian entrepreneurs who are actively looking for business opportunities abroad because they are completely unsure of the political situation and nature of government policy in the coming days. As a result, outward investment flows from India have become larger than inflow of foreign direct investment (FDI) in 2012-13! This trend of net positive outflow of investment from India is likely to not only continue but intensify as the policy paralysis and political instability take their toll in the coming months. This indeed is most unfortunate. This is happening because of an absence of any clear signals from any part of the political spectrum that their party will revert back to a policy regime of promoting investment, put down some strict and transparent governance norms and will not pander to populist pressures. When investors see the entire political class unable to take a stand against the food security bill, despite all that has been written about its weaknesses, they know it is time to cut their losses and look for opportunities elsewhere.

The direct consequence of the slowing down of economic growth and continued investment pessimism will be a further worsening of the employment prospects. This is already evident in the huge drop in the intake of students in second tier management schools and the drying up of job openings in the economy. One now hears of several cases where firms have stopped expanding their workforce and are just holding on (for a while only) before they begin to rationalise their workforce. Given that we need to create additional one million jobs each month (12 million new jobs every year) to keep pace with the expanding workforce, this drying up of employment can only mean rising frustration among the youth that will surely spill over into the streets and rapidly swell the ranks of the extremists of all hues. The rising Naxal violence and the audacious scale of their attacks could well reflect a growing sympathy for their cause among the young people who see a bleak future for themselves and are thoroughly dejected at the prospect of long term unemployment and the political class's complete apathy towards their cause.

The biggest irony is that no one in the leadership is willing to take the responsibility for this sorry state of economic affairs which could soon see the country plunge into social unrest and strife. The fact that while there have been several cabinet shuffles but not even one change in the team of economic managers or senior advisors probably demonstrates that the Prime Minister believes along with this advisors that nothing needs or can be done to improve the economic situation. This is shocking and reveals a continuing state of denial. Consequently, The UPA II has unfortunately wasted four years during which it could have put India on a double digit growth trajectory. Instead it has pandered to the worst forms of populism. It is indeed ironical that the Prime Minister who as Finance Minister wouldn't tire of telling us that India cannot afford competitive populism has presided over this sad turn of events.

The opposition on its part takes great delight in chastising the government and pointing to how the UPA II has brought the country from 9 per cent to less than 5 per cent rate of growth. But they must realise that their credibility is also hugely at stake. They cannot, I must add that they should not, expect to win the coming elections either in the four states or the centre only on the basis of a negative campaign targeted to highlight the government's failures. The opposition has to convince the electorate at this time that they will handle the economy more adroitly and with greater honesty and purpose. They have examples from Madhya Pradesh, Chhattisgarh and Gujarat to put forward. The people are tired of seeing them as nay-sayers. It is time that the BJP, being the principal opposition party, comes out with a well considered white paper on the economic situation in the country and how the party proposes to bring the country out of the present morass. A clearly enunciated economic road map that promotes investment and targets governance to improve equity and promises to work according to some universally recognised norms is the need of the hour.

6

Growth Not the Rupee Needs Attention

ACCORDING TO NEWSPAPER reports this morning, the Prime Minister was at pains to explain to the participants of a book release (essays in honour of Mr Chidambaram) function yesterday that India's GDP growth rate at 5.5 per cent for 2013-14 is not all that bad and certainly not a cause for alarm and emergency action. I do want to say that we will be lucky to get even 5 per cent GDP growth in 2013-14. But the reality is that there is a very downcast mood in the country today and repeated attempts by government economists to dispel the gloom and doom apparently leave everyone cold and unimpressed.

Perhaps this continued despondency is due not as much as to the economic slowdown, steep though as it is, but by the seeming inability of the government to engage with the issues at hand and lay down the way forward. The ongoing saga of the multi-brand retail policy; Vodafone case still hanging without a decision; Vedanta caught in a fix after spending more than a billion dollars; rising cases of corporate debt restructuring as even big established companies are suffering from the liquidity crunch etc. All these unresolved issues sap investors' confidence. The government needs to make some bold announcements to show that it is in control and on top of the situation. At present, however, the government seems adrift and as a result even the intrepid, perpetually opportunist Indian entrepreneur seems to have lost hope. Every investor I have met is currently in a wait and watch mode or actively pursuing opportunities abroad. That translates to a domestic investment famine which unfortunately implies no growth turnaround. May be the best bet at this stage is to end this lame duck condition of the government and not prolong the electoral process for the next nine months. Ongoing policy drift combined with increasing doses of populism could land our economy in a deep trough from which it may take a massive effort to bring it back on track.

The anti-growth trend was reinforced by the series of liquidity tightening steps, which the RBI took between the 15th to the 25th of July. In essence these steps, which are in line with the classic monetary policy response to check currency depreciation, represent RBI's effort to stabilise the external value of the currency by raising interest rates. Given the multiple pressures on the Rupee and the structural weaknesses that have emerged in the economy, the RBI cannot and should not even attempt to defend the Rupee. The pressure on the Rupee are: weak exports and rising trade deficit which shows no sign of declining despite the slowdown in imports due to the sagging economic growth; hardening oil prices; massive demand for gold seen as an inflation hedge in a situation where retail inflation has remained in double digits and real estate prices having ballooned face a real risk of a sharp correction; rising debt capital inflows by the corporate sector and greater commodity intensity of our imports with coal imports now accounting for as much as 3 per cent of total imports and rising. Import of other commodities like oil, gas, fertilisers, edible oil etc., are also increasing not because of any marked increase in demand but on account of domestic capacities having not expanded during the last five years. All these weaknesses are of course aggravated by the constant threat of a roll back of the US quantitative easing. Does the RBI really believe it can stabilise the Rupee at present levels in face of all these pressures?

How far is the RBI prepared to go in its defence of the currency? With the latest core sector data, released yesterday, showing a further weakening of growth (core sector growth was barely 0.1 per cent in the first quarter of this year ending June 30) impulses, it is not at all improbable to expect GDP growth to be well below 5 per cent in 2013-14. With a further tightening of liquidity in the domestic market, as a result of recent RBI measures, and a hike in the cost of capital, GDP growth would decline even more precipitously. We may end up in the same situation as in 2001 to 2003 when GDP growth had stalled in the wake of the dotcom crisis and high interest rate regime and fell to 3.8 per cent in 2003-04.

We cannot afford that kind of a slump in growth rates at this time in order to rein in inflation and stabilise the Rupee? We have to find a way forward and not throw up our hands as the RBI seems to have done while releasing its latest policy review and effectively admitting that it is unable to navigate through the trilemma. For a start, RBI would do well to give up its currency defence, unless they are aware of some hidden dangers that would result in a haemorrhaging of our reserves and/or put Rupee in a free fall. The worst possible outcome would be a somewhat undervalued Rupee for a period. That is not such a bad outcome as it will encourage consumption restraint and give our exporters and workers abroad much needed incentive to do better. As the RBI knows only too well by now, retail inflation in the county cannot be tamed by monetary measures, as it is clearly a supply side phenomenon, resulting from real wage increases, shortage of proteins and inadequate supply expansion in intermediate inputs like coal, fertilisers etc.

Today, India's GDP growth rate is lower and our retail inflation higher than that of Bangladesh and Sub-Saharan Africa. This should spur us to some real action rather than repeatedly asserting that we are still doing better than the advanced economies.

7

Economy: No Recovery in Sight

THERE ARE BY now a fairly large number of estimates for GDP growth in 2013-14. The *Economic Survey* gave a range between 6.1-6.7 per cent with Budget probably using 6.5 per cent. The Prime Minister's Economic Council has lowered its estimates to still improbable 6.4 per cent and the RBI has come out with its own lower forecast of 5.7 per cent. This is the same as that of the IMF. The ADB has estimated GDP growth in 2013-14 at 6 per cent and domestic think tanks and industry associations have come up with a range of estimates between 6.0-6.4 per cent. All these estimates, therefore, imply the beginning of a recovery, mild as it may be, and a 'bottoming out of the economy, which as we know hit a 10 year low of 5 per cent GDP growth rate in 2012-13. Given the performance in the first two years, the Planning Commission would do well to come up with a new set of numbers so that investment decisions are made on more reliable data and on realistic grounds.

Most estimates agree on agriculture growth being around 3 per cent, rising from the present year's low of 1.75 per cent. Industrial sector growth is generally pegged at 4.5 per cent in 2013-14, which again is higher than the very anaemic 3 per cent achieved in the last fiscal. Given their share in the GDP of about 12 and 28 per cent respectively, growth in these two sectors would yield a GDP growth of 1.62 per cent. Thus, as always the major contribution to GDP growth is assumed to come from the Services sector (including construction) which has a whopping share of 60 per cent in the GDP. The general assumption seems to be that its growth rate will rise to above 7.0 per cent in 2013-14 with some estimates putting it as high as 7.7 per cent as compared to 6.6 per cent in 2012-13. Thus, a recovery is premised on a better performance of the services sector.

The news on the services sector's prospects for 2013-14 is unfortunately not good. The latest HSBC PMI (Purchasing Managers Index) for services sector shows it to be declining to an 18 month low of 50.4 from 51.3 in October 2012. This does not indicate a better performance in 2013-14 as compared to the previous year. Also it should be noted that a PMI below 50 indicates an actual contraction in the sector. So according to this indicator the services sector may just achieve a positive growth rate and no where near 7 per cent as assumed by the forecasters. This is corroborated by several other indicators and anecdotal evidence. Growth in tourist arrivals, which declined to 2.9 per cent in 2012-13 from 6.7 per cent in 2011-12, is from all accounts set to weaken further and there are news of widespread vacancies in hotels and poor bookings for the coming winter season. Automobile sales (not car production) declined to 2.6 per cent in 2012-13 from as high as 11.0 per cent in 2011-12. These also show no signs at all of picking up with the demand in the first two months of the current fiscal remaining very weak. Domestic and international cargo movement, which had increased by 24 per cent in 2010-11, then contracted by 5 per cent in 2011-12 and again by negative 3 per cent in 2012-13. This is also not likely to increase much as world trade growth remains weak and India's own foreign trade is unlikely to regain its buoyancy of past years.

The two traditional drivers of services sector growth have been the telecom and financial sub-sectors. The telecom sector, which had seen growth rates of above 25 per cent year on year, seems to have run out of steam with significant contributions from the policy confusion contributing to this slowdown. Financial sector growth is hugely dependent on growth of major projects that need bank financing and on trade financing as well. According to data published by the RBI, the number of institutionally assisted projects came down from 543 in 2010-11 to 499 in 2012-13 and to a miserable low of 277 in the last fiscal year. The total cost (proxy for credit requirement) of these projects declined to a mere ₹911 billion in 2012-13 from a high of ₹3,104 billion in 2010-11. This huge fall is unlikely to be made up in the present year because from all accounts, there are no major projects being announced both in the manufacturing and indeed in the infrastructure sector as well. Lastly, a major sub-sector is community services along with other services offered by the public sector. These are unlikely to show any growth because of the pressure to reduce public expenditure and bring fiscal deficit under control. In the construction sector, there is hardly any signs of fresh buoyancy. Rental in metro cities are beginning to soften. Tier one and tier two cities are seeing some growth but much weaker as growth of commercial properties (read malls!) is reportedly weakening all over the country.

This detailed examination of the services sector prospects has been necessary to nail down the facile assumption made by a majority of forecasters that services sector growth, the mainstay of our economic growth, will pick up in the current year. On the basis of above, admittedly non-rigorous examination, I beg to differ. In my view, we will be lucky if the services sector growth remains at the same level (6.6%) as last year and it may well decline. If services sector growth (we are still not talking about a contraction or decline) is confined to 5.0 per cent in 2013-14, overall GDP growth will only be 4.6 per cent. Even if the services sector grows by the same rate as it did in 2012-13 (a low probability), it will yield an overall GDP growth of 5.5 per cent. Thus, my estimates for economic growth in 2013-14 range between 4.6-5.5 per cent. And this does not indicate any recovery or bottoming out. Most unfortunately, neither the government nor the main opposition parties are seized of this continued 'slowflation' in the economy. Its social consequences can be quite disastrous as employment opportunities dry up and the young people take to the streets and fuel the growth of extremist and lumpen violence in the country. It is time to take our attention away from scams and focus on the challenge of generating jobs and growth in the country.

8

Time for Hard and Right Decisions

BY THE TIME this column appears, the die may well have been cast with the RBI having made up its mind on the monetary policy action to be announced on Monday 2nd May. I only hope that it has not been unduly influenced by the monetary hawks especially those who use the wrong kind of data. The most commonly used and publicly discussed inflation data is the aggregate wholesale price (WPI) index as measured on a year on year (YOY) basis. The aggregate WPI includes the relatively volatile and seasonal fuel and food prices, and also trading margins that are also notoriously fickle. Therefore, economists tend to look at the core component of WPI which excludes food and fuel prices to get a better perspective of actual inflationary pressures. All over the world producers prices that reflect the ex-factory prices (and do not include trading margins) are used for measuring inflation. In India, the closest we come to producers prices are the consumer prices for industrial workers (CPI-IW) from which we could exclude the food and fuel components to get a better idea of underlying inflationary pressures. Moreover, a month on month (MOM) measure of inflation, duly de-seasonalised gives us a forward looking measure that is more relevant for policy making.

It is revealing to compare the MOM (three month moving average) rates of WPI and CPI-IW for non-food manufactured goods inflation from January 2010 to March 2011 (until January 2011 for CPI which is the latest available). On first sight the two series look quite similar with the WPI for February 2011 at 1.12 per cent (13.4% annualised) and the January 2011 CPI-IW at 1.19 per cent (14.0% annualised). The two show not only similar but worryingly high inflation level, which according to the hawks, provides more than sufficient basis for hiking up interest rates and by as much as 50 basis points to stay ahead of the inflationary curve and squeeze out inflationary expectations. But if we look closely at the two series, the crucial difference becomes clear. The MOM index for WPI has an upward tendency and gives a clear signal for an interest rate hike. But the CPI-IW is unambiguously on a downward trend having peaked in December 2009 at 2.0 per cent. This is important because if retail consumer prices have already peaked and are now declining as the MOM series clearly reflects, it is not only unnecessary but could be a serious mistake for the RBI to tighten monetary screws further. This would engender a sharp slowdown in growth as happened in the latter nineties after the interest rates were raised to nearly 12 per cent in 1996. The economy took more than five years to revert back to a high growth trajectory. We can least afford such a downward growth spiral at this time, when aspirations are soaring and the pressure of young entrants to the workforce is mounting relentlessly.

In can be argued that we cannot ignore rise in food and fuel prices. But as we know food prices are already declining and the expected bumper *Rabi* harvest will ensure that domestic food prices remain soft despite the global agriculture situation being expected to be somewhat precarious this year. The first monsoon forecast also augurs well for the *Kharif* crop. Thankfully, we look safe on the food front except for market rigidities. These are eminently amenable to policy correction like delisting perishables from the APMC (Agricultural Produce Market Committee) schedules that will in one stroke demolish the oligopolistic cartels that make huge speculative gains from minor supply disruptions. State governments should take this step urgently.

Crude oil prices are now at $120 per barrel and likely to be sticky given the searing energy demand from large emerging economies like the BRICS. A hike in interest rates is most unlikely to bring down domestic petroleum demand and prices. Instead the only way to curb rising hydrocarbon demand is to allow domestic petroleum prices to move in tandem with global prices. Domestic petrol, diesel and cooking gas prices must be decontrolled immediately. This will help rein in consumption and more importantly not allow suppressed inflationary pressures in this sector to vitiate prices and resource allocations elsewhere in the economy. RBI must insist that the government plays its due role in fighting inflation by taking this step and by announcing a cut in fertiliser and food subsidies. These subsidies like the kerosene subsidy, do not really benefit the poor and only feed corruption. A bold announcement for a sharper and quicker reduction in revenue deficit and a smaller public sector borrowing programme will tend to soften market interest rates which would be a clear signal to investors that the government is prepared to play its due role in achieving macroeconomic stability. Relying exclusively on monetary policy to achieve macroeconomic stability may well be the wrong medicine at this time. We need to expand capacities in the manufacturing sector and raise investment demand rather than hold back private consumption. An interest rate hike without corresponding fiscal action could lead us to a precipitate decline in growth from which the economy may well take several years to come out. That will be economically suicidal and could have political implications as well.

9

The 2013-14 Budget

Workmanlike and May Have Missed an Opportunity

GIVEN HIS REPUTATION, Mr Chidambaram had raised high expectations. Faced with an economic slowdown, bad both for the economy as also for UPA's electoral prospects, he was indeed brought in to handle a tough situation. He could have used his reputation and the common perception that the country is faced with a significant economic crisis to strike out boldly and push the reform agenda. His preamble to the budget proposals raised those hopes. He recognised that the investment sentiment was at its weakest and needed a real push. He emphasised that the current account deficit (CAD) was even a bigger problem than the formidable challenge of containing the fiscal deficit and pursuing the fiscal road map as recommended by the Kelkar committee. In the end, however, the finance minister opted for being cautious and workmanlike and to try and please one and all. Could it be that in doing so he has missed an opportunity to bring back real dynamism to the Indian economy?

Nonetheless, some will argue that he almost lived up to his formidable reputation of being a miracle man and pulling the economy out of trouble and restarting the investment engine. To this end, he has announced an additional 15 per cent investment allowance for the next two years in an attempt to shore up the investment sentiment. He has further done extensive tinkering in allocating ₹2,400 crore for the textile industry's technology upgrading fund; by providing for issuance of tax free bonds up to ₹50,000 crore for infrastructure projects; doubling the capital available to SIDBI; permitting the MSMEs to avail of non-tax benefits for three years after they have graduated from their MSME status; and pushing back the implementation of GARR to 2016-17. All this is very well but does this go far enough to arouse the near dormant animal spirits? Time will tell. But the first signs from the markets are that investors are not impressed. This is perhaps because these investment promotion measures have been offset by the hike in corporate income and the dividend distribution tax and the 10 per cent surcharge on the super rich. And he did not roll back the retrospective tax law that caused so much consternation last year. Combined with the higher excise duties on the SUVs and the lack of any measure to strengthen demand for consumer durables, the production of which has been plummeting in recent months, there is not much left to cheer for the investors. So we may not see the rebound in investment that is critical to get the economic growth back on a higher trajectory.

On controlling the fiscal deficit, the finance minister has ostensibly kept his promise of containing the fiscal deficit to less than 5.3 per cent in 2012-13 and bringing it down to 4.8 per cent of the GDP in 2013-14. However, to achieve this, the subsidy bill is estimated to decline from ₹2,57,654 crore in the revised estimates for 2012-13 to ₹2,31,084 crore in 2013-14 or a reduction of more than 10 per cent in the total subsidy amount. Total subsidies are stipulated to come down from 2.6 per cent of the GDP in 2012-13 to 2.0 per cent in the next fiscal. This would indeed be very challenging given that he has allocated only an additional ₹10,000 crore for financing the food security bill, which will be pushed by the UPA to improve its electoral prospects. Moreover, the petroleum subsidy bill is estimated to decline by more than ₹31,000 crore or by nearly 30 per cent compared to 2012-13. This must be based on a continuing hike in diesel and petroleum prices. I hope this effective de-control of petroleum prices is implemented as the pressures to roll it back, and hence to increase the subsidy, will be considerable in an election year, especially when the WPI based inflation rate, according to the assumptions made in the budget itself, is expected to remain at 7 per cent and the CPI based inflation will remain elevated to nearly double digits. The reduction in 2013-14 fiscal deficit is also based on a high disinvestment plan of ₹55,800 crore. The feasibility of achieving this rather ambitious target is questionable. Here again, given the opportunity, the finance minister could have taken the axe to a whole gamut of unnecessary public expenditure, of which he is well aware and insisted on implementing an outcome based budgeting that he had himself earlier initiated. I only hope that the rating agencies will accept his estimates and not act adversely.

On reducing the current account deficit (CAD), the budget seems to have approached it from the angle of raising domestic savings rather than improving foreign capital flows or aggressively increasing exports. To increase household savings, the cap for equity investments under the RGS Saving Scheme has been raised and inflation indexed bonds will be issued later after consultations with the RBI. The budget does not try to reduce government dis-savings and bring down the revenue deficit more aggressively. In fact government expenditure is estimated to rise by 16.4 per cent in 2013-14 as compared to 9.7 per cent in 2012-13, thereby raising public expenditure to 14.7 per cent of GDP in FY 14 as compared to 14.3 per cent in FY 13. This implies an even bigger government at a time when austerity was required. Other measures to lower the CAD like improving the competitiveness of our exports, or reducing energy imports by incentivising energy conservation or reducing gold imports are missing from the budget. Let us hope that the foreign trade policy to be announced in March will have some strong and innovative measures for reversing the current decline in exports, which we cannot afford.

It is not a bad budget by any means. It is workmanlike, balanced and the finance minister has done well not succumb to electoral pressures, though he has made the symbolic gestures to the three electoral constituencies of women, youth and the poor. But given that in our country a crisis represents the best opportunity for pushing forward with urgent and necessary reforms, he may have missed an opportunity to qualitatively improve economic governance including the delivery of public services and made the climate more investment friendly. The attempt to balance economic priorities against political expediency has apparently resulted in a virtual standstill on the reform agenda. Let us hope this does not have adverse longer term consequences.

10

On Thin Ice

Vote on Account 2014-15

I WISH MR P. CHIDAMBARAM (PC) was less predictable today in presenting the vote on account. That would have encouraged him to accept that the country is in some serious economic trouble which would require sincere bipartisan effort to bring it back to the desired growth trajectory. Instead, true to his and this government's self-congratulatory form, he asserted that he has not only achieved macroeconomic stability in the 17 months he has been Finance Minister, a major task in itself, but also engineered an economic growth recovery. He is on thin ice on all counts. Central Statistical Organisation (CSO) has been optimistic in estimating 2013-14 GDP growth at 4.9 per cent after achieving only 4.6 per cent in the first half of 2013-14. On this basis the finance minister assumes that the growth in the second half will be higher at 5.2 per cent and so announced the start of an economic recovery. But he must know that that final private consumption growth will moderate to 4.1 per cent in 2013-14 as compared to 5.0 per cent in the previous year and gross fixed capital formation (GFCF) will be stagnant at 0.2 per cent after a measly growth of 0.8 per cent in 2012-13. Imports continue to decline reflecting weak domestic demand; industrial growth has been negative in October and November and manufacturing is expected to shrink this year. All these indicators do not point to a above 5 per cent growth in the second half of 2013-14. And, economic growth in 2014-15 will surely not be above 7 per cent as seems to have been assumed in projecting nominal GDP growth to be above 13 per cent for next year.

The finance minister has overcome the revenue shortfall of nearly ₹75,000 crore by ferociously axing plan expenditure by ₹79,790 crore. Of this, about ₹8,000 crore has been cut on the capital account and the rest on plan revenue expenditure. Non-plan expenditure has been marginally increased by ₹5,000 crore which implies a lower outlay on real sectors as interest payments have gone up by ₹9,000 crore. More worrying aspect is a cut of ₹30,000 crore on non-plan capital expenditure. Thus, the finance minister has not hesitated to impair the productive capacities of the economy while increasing subsidy payments by ₹24,000 crore and pushing ₹35,000 crore of oil subsidies to be paid next year. It is widely reported that a significant volume of expenditure incurred within this fiscal year, has been pushed forward for the next year and tax refunds have also been held back. On fiscal deficit, therefore, the quality of adjustment made to 'over achieve' the target leaves much to be desired.

The current account deficit is expected to come down to 2.5 per cent of the GDP. However, it should be noted that this has come about with a drastic decline in imports of 16.7 per cent between September and January 2014 and by 7.4 per cent in the 10 months of the current fiscal. Gold imports have gone down dramatically (80% decline between September to November and 25% since April) but from all accounts, gold smuggling has increased and threatens to revert back to pre-1994 days. To have achieved an external account balance by these means is hardly sustainable and does not augur well for the future.

So on all three counts of growth, fiscal deficit and external account management, the achievements are not entirely kosher. It would therefore be dangerous to declare victory and become complacent. In fact the next government will probably inherit an economy that is still very much in the downswing and macroeconomic situation precariously balanced. Would it not have brought greater credit to him, if PC showed even a modest degree of contrition on behalf of the UPA for the current economic malaise and admitted to not having followed his own 10 dictums for good macroeconomic management that he so eloquently espoused during the speech. It is surely worth reminding him that it was under his watch in February 2008 that all fiscal norms were brazenly flouted and the fiscal deficit allowed to jump up from 2.5 per cent of GDP in 2007-08 to a whopping 6.0 per cent in 2008-09. And this was done ahead of the global financial crisis! That one major act of politically expedient fiscal profligacy perhaps started the process that has brought the economy to its present dismal condition.

The finance minister has done well to reduce the excise duties on the automobile sector which has seen output decline for longer than at any other time one can remember. He has also reduced the excise duties on some capital goods, which have seen massive decline in output in this year. Reduction in excise duties on automobiles will hopefully help reverse the steep decline in demand but let us not count on that given the pessimistic mood of the consumers faced with income and employment stagnation. It is noteworthy that he has not used this opportunity to announce some new schemes to gain electoral advantage. That I suppose would have been quite contrary to the conventions of presenting a vote on account. But some observers have felt that in recounting the 10 year achievements of this government and in laying down some excise and other duty cuts for next year, he may have still overstepped his constitutional mandate

Overall, this was a typical combative display by the finance minister known for his combativeness and eye on detail. This was very much reflected in the numbers he reeled out for the 24 sector skill councils that have been established or the 12.5 lakh land titles handed out or indeed the approval for establishing two semi-conductor wafer labs. How one wished that PC, whom I have known for nearly three decades, had boldly risen above his partisan position and used his swan song to emerge as a statesman to whom the country could look up to in the difficult times that lie ahead.

11

Eleven Big Ideas for 2014

TALKING OF BIG IDEAS for 2014 assumes that the political environment after general elections in April-May 2014 will be conducive to long term and strategic policy making, necessary for implementing new and bold ideas. Politicians obsessed with retaining power, are happy with the status quo, which affords them maximum time for manipulative politics and rent-maximisation.

Therefore, let us hope that the Indian electorate will, as in the past, surprise us all and deliver a clear and unambiguous electoral verdict in 2014 that in favour of a decisive and stable government with a leadership that thinks beyond retention of power, pursues an agenda for national resurgence and is capable of taking decisions and having them implemented. A tall order perhaps but one that is critically needed at this time. Eleven bold steps required to put India on the path of sustained and inclusive high growth are discussed as follows.

First, abolish all current household and individual targeted subsidies, including the food subsidy, and replace them by a conditional cash transfer scheme. The cash will be deposited in the bank account of the female head of the beneficiary household. The eligibility criteria will be that households ensure that all children below the age of 16, especially daughters, are in school. NREGA will also be done away with once these conditional cash transfers are in place.

Second, maximum flexibility in labour markets to be achieved by establishing a labour welfare fund (with equal contributions by employers and government) that will finance transitory unemployment and re-training. This is necessary to eliminate poverty for which doles will not suffice. Instead we need to generate 20 million new jobs in the next 10 years by accelerating growth in labour intensive industries like tourism, handicrafts, mass manufacturing of garments and light engineering products. For these industries to prosper, we need labour market flexibility.

Third, do away with the plethora of clearance and compliances required by the harried investor and combine all these nearly 70 clearances into one comprehensive form which requires to be submitted only once. This alone will make the 'single window clearance' a reality and not a mere slogan. We must realise that poverty will not be eliminated unless the rate of growth of the manufacturing sector is accelerated to a minimum of 12 per cent per annum. The necessary condition for this is a conducive investment environment, which will be achieved by combining the 70 odd clearances in one comprehensive form.

Fourth, continuing with focus on manufacturing and more specifically on MSMEs, it is imperative to minimise if not eliminate the visits of any inspector under the Factories Act for units employing less than 200 workers. Freeing the MSMEs from the tyranny of the 'inspector raj', not yet achieved despite all the rhetoric, will be a massive boost to our industrialisation and employment. This has to be accompanied by instituting a system of heavy penalties that act as a real deterrent for employer apprehended for not abiding by the minimum criteria for working conditions, pollution control and employment of child labour.

Fifth, thoroughly review and be prepared to jettison if necessary, the system of minimum support prices for food grains and other selected crops. This has, over the years, created massive distortions like rice cultivation in water scarce Punjab, disincentives against high value crops and made agriculture a high cost sector with minimal incentives for technology upgradation and productivity enhancement. It is time to unshackle Indian agriculture from government controls and intervention, and let the Indian farmer enjoy the benefit of his entrepreneurial dynamism. Agriculture sector will also greatly benefit by the immediate abolition of all subsidies for fertilisers and pesticides that have resulted in large scale soil degradation and raised toxic levels in food products.

Sixth, complete the four way division of Uttar Pradesh (UP) which is long overdue. The state with a population of 200 million and 60 odd districts is an administrative dead loss. There is huge heterogeneity across the four distinct regions which makes policy making extremely difficult if not impossible. The four new states comprising current districts in West UP, Oudh, Eastern UP and Bundelkhand will be far more manageable administratively and following the example of other smaller states achieve far better economic performance.

Seventh, India needs new monuments. One such could be the Kalpasar project proposed by the Gujarat government. It envisages building a 64 km dam across the Gulf of Khambat, connecting the two rivers, Ghogha and Hasnot, thereby creating a 2000 sq mile fresh water lake which will also generate 5880 MW of tidal energy and irrigate 1.05 million hectares of land in South Saurashtra. A mega-project of this nature will fire the imagination of this nation and reinvigorate our science and technology community.

Eighth, privatise Air India and all the hotels owned and managed either by the central or state governments or their agencies. Given the continuing financial haemorrhaging of these entities we can hardly afford them in a period of fiscal constraint. And selling them off will send the right signal to other public sector enterprises who should be required to earn a minimum 10 per cent return on the capital invested. It will also help to bring down the revenue deficit to zero, which in itself is a much needed measure to restore macroeconomic stability.

Ninth, introduce the PPP model in the health sector. This can be achieved by putting in place a regulatory framework that will ensure that all public health centres (PHCs) treat a minimum number of patients every day on government terms, but doctors can also use the premises after regular hours for private practice, charging commercial rates from patients who can afford to pay. This model could also be applied to government dispensaries and district hospitals, and could provide the balance between the crass commercialisation of private hospitals on the one hand and unacceptably poor patient treatment in government hospitals on the other.

Tenth, it is time to bring real dynamism into the Indian railways by breaking up this monolith into more nimble smaller independent regional units, corporatising all their ancillary operations like hospitals, schools and catering, and converting the Railway Board into exclusively a policy making body. This is long overdue and is perhaps the only way to reverse the declining trend in railway's share of both freight and passenger traffic.

Eleventh, the Ganges should be made navigable again from Kolkata to Kanpur as it once was. The sight of a large barge or steamer sailing up the Ganges past Kashi to Allahabad and Kanpur will reverse decades of cynicism and neglect towards our rivers and environment more generally.

This is indeed a formidable agenda for action. But is eminently achievable. If implemented it will not only bring India back to the high growth path but also usher in a period of competitive good governance that could propel India to achieve its true potential.

12

Nurturing the Sweet Spot

MR NARENDRA MODI is currently in an enviable sweet spot for any political leader. The Indian electorate is seeming to accept his credibility, credentials and claim for leading the next government. Consequently, he can publicly dismiss with disdain, as he did during his speech on the 27th at the India Foundation event in Delhi, Mr Chidambaram's demand for explaining his economic programme and understanding by asserting that his entire economic understanding could be put down on the back of a postage stamp and was summed up in one mantra that he borrowed from Mahatma Gandhi *viz.*, Trusteeship. It is a reflection of him currently occupying the political sweet spot that the audience made up of hard-nosed bankers, accountants, economists and assorted professionals, accepted that as sufficient and loudly cheered him when he added that he does not need more than that because he can hire professionals for any further technicalities. How do you think the same audience would react to a similar statement from the presently beleaguered Rahul Gandhi? He would be seen to be arrogant, underprepared and unfit to lead the economy back to a high growth trajectory without displaying profound and in-depth knowledge of economic issues. The difference I suppose arises from the very different track records that the two have built over the last 10 years—one seen to have delivered on his promises and the other to have betrayed the trust reposed in him and his party and merely offered angry rhetoric in place of actual outcomes. Try as much as he can, Rahul Gandhi cannot shrug away his party's record and nor should he be allowed to get away with it as he has been very much central to the party's and indeed government's decision-making and performance.

I am sure that Mr Modi is acutely aware of the dangers of complacency during this last lap of a long race that is tantalisingly nearing the finish. If we go by the polls some work still remains to be done. BJP's share of the total votes at about 29 per cent is already predicted to be at an all time high. But this may still not suffice to give Modi a clear mandate within his party and *vis-á-vis* the likely coalition partners to lead the government. For achieving that mandate, his vote share will have to be nearer or above the 35 per cent mark, which characterises a wave. To get towards that mark Mr Modi will have to warn his team against the risk of complacency that will increase exponentially as the indefatigable *durbaris* of the *Dilli Durbar* swell his entourage; sycophants hail him as the new *messiah*; crony capitalists sing his paeans and open their wallets at the same time; and servile *babus* with vested interests will swear allegiance to 'Modinomics'. This is already starting to happen and the danger is that with AAP trying its best to paint both the BJP and the Congress with the same brush, Modi will loose critically important vote share, as the BJP did in Delhi if he does not successfully portray himself as being an outsider to the *Dilli Durbar,* much as Obama so successfully did during his first campaign in 2008. It will be disastrous at this stage for the BJP to be seen as a duplicate version of the Congress party with both of them vying for power only to serve their narrow sectional interests or for maximising personal gains.

Mr Modi has quite visibly realised this need for sharply distinguishing himself from the run of the mill political leaders and this is reflected in several of his utterances. His repeated reference to *shasak nahin sewak* (one who serves and does not rule); maximum governance with minimum government; not rule making but rule implementation; are examples of this necessary product differentiation. He was bold in referring to the necessity for hard decision-making during his speech on the 26th. This is most welcome as we need to reverse the rampant populism that has been the UPA's creed for the last 10 years. I would like to assure Mr Modi that the electorate is not only prepared at this stage but in fact wanting more discipline in public life and will support hard decisions as long it can see that these are necessary for national resurgence. An example should suffice. The electorate will surely support him if he was to boldly talk about establishing stricter norms for public sector enterprises including defence enterprises and more decisive procurement decisions for strategic equipment. This will of course tread on the toes of a few thousand public sector employees but increase his credibility manifold in the large voting middle class and young population.

One other major step is necessary at this stage for Mr Modi to distinguish himself as being qualitatively different from the rest of the professional political class, which today is largely discredited. He will do well to take cognisance of recent media exposes of crony capitalists, including the latest one involving Sahara's Roy and of AAP's determined and no holds barred attempt at linking him with and the BJP with individual business leaders. This will only become shriller and sharper as the election approaches. It may be useful at this stage for Mr Modi to draw a sharp line and project himself as above any individual or sectional business interests. The electorate of course expects him to work for promoting manufacturing and private investment in the country. They also expect him to improve the business climate for attracting both domestic and foreign investment as that will generate the much needed employment and push up economic growth. So is it worth his while to now consider reiterating the decision that the BJP had taken some time back that contribution to the election funds will be taken only through cheques. And further that his mantra of rule based and not discretion based style of governance that he has established in Gujarat will be extended in all Central government ministries and departments within the first year of his taking office. This will take him closer to 35 per cent of the vote share and give India a clean break from the past.

13

Targeting Inflation with Price Rigidities

RBI TOOK THE MARKET by surprise by raising the repo rate by 0.25 per cent to 8 per cent. But to those who have followed the recommendations of the Urjit Patel Committee (UPC), the measure will be seen as consistent with the RBI's declared target of bringing headline CPI inflation to below 8 per cent, and within its comfort zone. As an 'inflation targeter' which is now its official position, the RBI, has with this move, tried to move ahead of the curve of inflationary expectations. Raising the interest rate is an attempt to signal to all relevant economic agents and more specifically those who set wages and prices of goods and services that RBI will not relent until it has inflation under control. RBI wants to emphasise that it sees high inflation as anti-growth. A stable inflation environment, according to the RBI, is a necessary condition for a turnaround in the rate of economic growth. At least we have a consistent story here and RBI should be commended staying the course that it has laid down for itself.

The obvious question is whether RBI's or UPC's understanding of the economy and the role of monetary policy in the rather complex ground realities in India is the right one. Headline CPI inflation has stubbornly remained above 9 per cent for the last 60 months with core retail inflation remaining above 8 per cent during this period. So it can be argued that persistent high inflation can co-exist with both high and low rates of economic growth in India. After all GDP growth during 2003-2009 averaged more that 7.5 per cent when inflation was high. And conversely, with the repo rate having been raised on four occasions in 2013 and GDP growth slowing down appreciably, inflation, especially retail inflation remains stubbornly high. I have tried to look for an analytical explanation of this apparent paradox in RBI's policy statements or the Governor's own speeches, but have missed it.

It can be argued that the persistence of high inflation despite the growth slowdown reflects that the gap between a declining demand and existing supply capacities remains wide and is not closing. This can only happen if the supply capacity of the economy (referred to by us economists as the rate of growth of potential output) is also declining. This is a serious and worrisome conclusion because it implies that in the last five years, government policies, or the lack of it, have actually degenerated our supply side capabilities. This could have been a result of for example driving down private investment; raising the incremental capital output ratio (ICOR) by locking up capital in un-productive or non-functioning projects; or driving down labour productivity by not generating higher output from the existing labour stock whose nominal wages rise in line with inflation. Could it be that the rise in interest rates, by raising the cost of capital and demonstrating an anti-growth bias, could further also contribute to the decline in the rate of growth of potential output? This would be reflected in investors choosing to invest abroad to escape the high cost of capital and policy uncertainties.

There is, however, a broader issue about the RBI becoming an 'inflation targeter' in an economy in which large parts of the economy are characterised by price rigidities and mark-up pricing. Intermediate sectors like coal, diesel, electricity and others which have direct impact on downstream costs and prices are fixed and controlled by government fiat. Similarly, a large number of agriculture prices that cover nearly 30 per cent of agro output including all major cereals and sugarcane are also administratively fixed. Unfortunately, these prices are not and will not be affected by a softening of demand. Instead, the rise in capital costs enters the price fixation formulae and results in ratcheting up these prices irrespective of the demand-supply balance. Raising interest rates could in these conditions have a perverse outcome.

Nonetheless, it is clear that by persisting with its anti-inflation stance, the RBI is signalling sharply that policy measures are urgently needed to improve supply capabilities to raise the rate of growth of potential output. These include the oft mentioned measures of removing structural impediments in the inter-state movement of agriculture produce; eliminating monopoly control of critical intermediate sectors like coal; raising public investment in productivity enhancing schemes in agriculture; addressing the debilitating infrastructure deficit that makes it impossible for our SMEs to face import competition; improving governance especially in the allocation of natural resources while establishing a transparent and efficient regulatory framework; and reducing the revenue deficit, which inevitably raises the costs of credit and effectively pre-empts private investment.

These measures should have been taken in the last 10 years but were not. This represent a hugely missed opportunity to achieve sustained high GDP growth rates with a balanced macroeconomic structure. Contrary to what the Finance Ministry has stated, economic growth does not necessarily have to be cyclical or volatile. This has been amply and persistently demonstrated over the last three decades by China. I am sure that if the Chinese could manage three decades of sustained rapid economic growth, India can too. For that we will have to be far more steeped into our own complex realities and not simply imitate paradigms borrowed from advanced economies and try and fit our reality into them. Monetary policy by itself is constrained by its limited arsenal of policy instruments. It can hardly be expected to yield both high growth, lower inflation and exchange rate stability at the same time. Surely it cannot also be allowed to become dogmatic and lose the much needed flexibility to effectively respond to issues that arise in as complex an economy like India that is characterised by price rigidities and discontinuous behaviour of critical parameters.

14

Reserve Bank of India: Nothing New

RBI's POLICY ANNOUNCEMENT on 29th October carried no surprises. Repo rates were raised by 0.25 basis points and rates at which commercial banks can borrow under the marginal standing facility were lowered by the same amount. Normalcy was brought back in the money markets with the LAF corridor brought back to within 100 basis points. The yield curve regains its 'normal shape' and all this was applauded by the equity markets, with the Sensex closing 355 points above the previous day. I notice, however, that several commentators and edits have risked being chided as spoil sports by pointing out that markets are perhaps being irrationally exuberant.

The Governor has demonstrated most unambiguously that his exclusive objective for now is to tame inflation. He wants to dampen inflationary expectations that showed a marked rise during the July-September period before they become more deeply entrenched. Therefore, he has shifted his attention to retail inflation (CPI), which has remained around 8 per cent for the past 60 months, with core retail inflation at 7-8 per cent and food inflation above 10 per cent. By overtly focusing on CPI as the basis for policy stance, he is following a well worn RBI practice of using a mix of retail inflation measures, but which has not generally been openly admitted. Will interest rate hikes, cheered along as always by the Chairman of the Prime Minister's Economic Advisory Council, Dr Rangarajan, by themselves suffice to reverse inflationary expectations after 60 months and will the economy not suffer inordinately during the ensuing period? The analogy with chemotherapy, to which my family has been unfortunately recently exposed, is an apt one. The oncologist is sure that if a strong enough dose is administered long enough, the malignancy will be rooted out from the system. But often he/she stops short or staggers the dosage because sustained chemotherapy not only kills both malignant and benign cells, but also risks destroying the bone marrow, thereby rendering the system completely incapable of positive response.

With credit growth slowing down to 11-12 per cent; consumption and investment demand both lower than in comparable periods in the previous year; and political uncertainty bringing private investment to a standstill and looming ominously on the investment sentiments, one wonders if the economic system's bone marrow in not already displaying signs of being near comatose? Perhaps the Governor, like some doctors, prefers taking the risk of pushing the patient in to the exclusion ICU, used for patients with immunity levels, before acting. The danger always is that even if yanked back from the precipice, the patient, in this case the economy, becomes crippled for a long time. The governor seems to believe that downside risks for growth, reflected in his optimist growth forecast of 5 per cent, are still manageable but the upside risks of rising inflationary expectations are getting out of hand.

I beg to differ, because rate hikes will do precious little to curb inflation that is fuelled by shortages of non-cereal food supplies and burgeoning fiscal deficit. The government now fully in election mode; 75 per cent of the fiscal deficit target already exhausted in the first eight months; and tax revenues significantly lower than planned, there is virtually no hope whatsoever for reducing the government borrowing requirement except through imaginative accounting, which will not help in any case. But defenders of inflation targeting argue that the RBI can do precious little as structural constraints on growth, supply shortages and fiscal profligacy are out of its hands. It has only a single policy variable to play with. Well that is assuming that Mint Road and North Block cannot be in sync. We cannot expect a coherent a government policy that uses all feasible tools to minimise the chemotherapy and prevent the system from going into the ICU, from which it takes a long time to recover and heavy costs are incurred in terms of investment famine, plummeting growth and massive job losses.

The hope was that Raghuram Rajan, having served as the Prime Minister's special economic advisor for several years and as the chief economic advisor in North Block would bring to policy making this hitherto missing dimension of overall macro policy coherence. This would have implied that in between the two RBI policy announcements, the government would have taken real steps to address those structural constraints by simplifying environment clearance and not passing the LARR, rein in fiscal deficit by removing the diesel subsidy and not passing the FSB; or taking steps to reduce the criminal waste of 40 per cent of agriculture produce (as reported by the UK based Institute of Mechanical Engineers recently) or eliminate brazen and open cartelisation in the wholesale fruits and vegetables markets by abolishing the APMC act in UPA ruled states.

But none of that has happened. So what is new that the Governor brings to the table of policy making apart from his global reputation. We are back on the macroeconomic roller coaster propelled upwards on the inflationary spiral by a loose fiscal regime and lack of policy response to supply side bottlenecks and hurtling down by ever tightening monetary policy. This scenario is to the utter delight of the hide bound monetarists. They can show their policy muscle by stopping growth in its tracks to achieve an inflation target.

But a Governor more sensitive to the social pains of job losses and large scale shutting down of small and medium enterprises, that are unable to withstand the double whammy of interest hikes and higher input costs, would have acted differently. He would have used his convincing powers, coalition building skills and intervention in the public domain to bring about the much needed policy coherence and forcing North Block to come up with real action in place of rhetoric. Instead there seems to be the usual capitulation to political compulsions. The Governor seems happy enough receiving accolades from equity brokers, FIIs and foreign bankers. But surely the Governor realises that the markets are making the proverbial 'dead cat jump' because there is precious little to sustain this euphoria. Come the next quarter's GDP growth numbers or even a hint of tapering by the US Fed around the new year and markets will be in deep funk again.

By being the inflation hawk, Raghu is playing to a well-known script, which does not include sustained growth with low inflation, critically needed today. We were all expecting something different.

15

Christening by Fire and an Opportunity Not to Be Missed

THIS IS INDEED a christening by fire for Dr Raghuram Rajan as he steps into the top job at Mint Road. Growth and employment are falling; retail inflation remains stubbornly high in double digits for the last 60 months! And to complete the trilemma, the current account deficit (CAD) threatens to remain above 4 per cent and the Rupee, having declined 15 per cent in the last three months, seems to be in danger of getting into a free fall despite the incredible rise on Friday, 23 August. It really couldn't get tougher for an incoming Governor.

Going by his amazing credentials, there could hardly be anyone better equipped to take on this challenge and moreover because he has also authored a full-fledged report on the Indian financial sector reforms that would have given him a first-hand feel of the issues, challenges and reforms for the banking and financial sector. There are not too many people who are given the opportunity to implement what they have preached. And so the Governor should simply go for implementing his own recommendations and liberalise the banking and financial sector; introduce an arms-length regulation with a lighter touch; make RBI a more market friendly regulator and consolidate fragmented capacities that presently characterise this sector. These reforms have long been in waiting and need immediate attention.

The 'minor hurdle' he has to overcome before he can get down to implementing these reforms is to stop the ongoing haemorrhaging of the external account, halt the slide in Rupee's value, and get the economy out of its downturn which threatens to become long and deep. At the present juncture, this may not be easy even for a man with his talents, because the task will presumably become even tougher as the electoral cycle enters its final phase and populist pressures become unrelenting. I wonder about his response when he suddenly finds that his former bosses and colleagues in North Block or across the road in the PMO do not agree with either his diagnosis or prescriptions or both. The gulf between Mint Road and Raisina Hill is often far more than mere geographical distance. They can be poles apart. He would require all his skills at coalition building to get the job done. Lets hope that having worked in the IMF and as PM's special advisor should have given him persuasion and coalition building skills as well.

The first step in bringing back macroeconomic management to some order would be for him to admit that the economy is in crisis and better still show some contrition on behalf of all his former and present colleagues who have persisted in their denial of such a crisis. A straight forward *mea culpa* would begin to restore the credibility of the government, which today is at its nadir. He can afford to do this because he is one step removed from party politics, does not have to face irate and partisan MPs in the parliament and as a technocrat is expected to exclusively safeguard the country's economic health. To continue blaming external conditions will only worsen the situation.

Second, he would do well to strongly advocate structural reforms that are needed today to restore investors' confidence and stop the capital flight as reflected in the continuing demand for gold despite the imposition of the 10 per cent import duty. While major confidence restoring measures lie outside his mandate, he should cajole and plead with North Block and other ministries to do the right things. He should appear to be reading from the same script as the finance minister and his former colleagues, because any spat, even if minor, between North Block and Mint Road causes avoidable confusion and impairs investors' confidence. However, he will do well to maintain his distance from Vigyan Bhawan annex from where he will only hear calls for clamping down on aggregate demand to bring inflation down below 5 per cent even it that results in the economy's demise.

A point for him to note would that be RBI's permission for banks to hold until maturity government 10 years securities for SLR, rather than mark them to market, combined with some open market purchases brought immediate relief to the market and did a lot to dispel the sense of deepening crisis in financial markets. So perhaps further liberalisation is required rather than continued demand repression. There are several arrows in the monetary policy quiver that can be used to signal that government is serious about restoring growth and one of them could be to reduce the CRR and encourage banks to reverse interest rate hikes and start disbursing credit. He should be aware that some banks are presently hoarding liquidity and not releasing credit even against sanctioned amounts causing undue stress.

Third, he may want to look at some rather nitty-gritty measures that will bring in investment into the priority sectors, which have strong multiplier effects. For example, the proposal for permitting housing finance companies to access long term external commercial borrowings was hanging fire for 11 years. One year ago it was cleared but the NBFCs that applied for such ECB access have seen their applications shuttling between the RBI and the National Housing Bank, and clearance is still awaited!! What a pity indeed as bringing long term dollars in to the housing finance sectors, of course with all due prudential regulations, would have multiple beneficial effects on investment, growth and employment.

Fourth, it is perhaps too much of a minutiae for the governor to know that while commercial banks are allowed to include housing loans of up to ₹25 lakh per loan in their priority sector lending, this limit comes down to ₹10 lakh when the banks do so by off-loading the lending to NBFCs, which nearly all commercial banks do because the NBFCs are more efficient at disbursing these lower value home loans. Further, education loans are not included in the priority sector at all if given through the NBFCs. These anomalies need to be done away with and it is time the RBI extricated itself from such micro-management of the banking sector.

Fifth, it is not clear to me why the RBI should be running its own banking subsidiaries. This surely dilutes its attention from regulatory and monetary policy responsibilities. While he is divesting RBI's holdings in these banks, he may as well recall RBI's representative from the SBI's Board of Directors, even if the outdated SBI Act requires it. I have observed this anomaly for the past five years and seen corporate governance in the largest commercial bank becoming a bit of a shadow play. What else could one expect when the owner of the SBI represented by Secretary, Financial Services and the regulator (Deputy Governor RBI) are both present on the Board! The remaining independent directors simply don't matter even if they tried. Most give up fairly early anyway. I am sure this is true of other commercial banks as well. Raghu would do well to improve corporate governance in the banking and financial sector to set the right tone for the new banks.

Perhaps it is time also for him to push really hard to have the amendment in the banking sector law that precludes government share from coming down below 51 per cent in public sector banks. Is it not in line with his own recommendations from an earlier avatar? This is quite an agenda for the incoming Governor to handle but lets hope he will rise to the task. A lot is riding on that.

16

Well Begun but Not Quite Half Done

MARKETS HAVE CHEERED Raghuram Rajan's arrival at the RBI. True to our expectations and in keeping with his reputation, Raghu has hit the deck running and announced a slew of measures, which reflect solid thinking and preparation. As I had said in an earlier piece, he is one of the few lucky persons who gets to implement what he has recommended and it is heartening to see that in his opening speech, Raghu has not flinched from owning his own report and quoted from it on the issue of Electronic Bill Factoring for MSMEs. This conveys that he will move in the direction of steadily liberalising the banking sector and modernising financial sector management in the country. This should have happened years ago but better late than never. Lets hope that the committees being set up by the Governor will suggest fresh measures for the conduct of monetary policy, more transparent and effective ways of handling the non-performing assets (NPAs) by commercial banks and some innovative means for improving financial inclusion in the country.

The suggestion to reduce the quantum of government securities required to be held by the bank is indeed a welcome one. But as he has himself admitted this will take time to materialise, dependent as it is on the reduction in the government's borrowing requirements. Available data tells us that 63.2 per cent of the fiscal deficit target has already been exhausted in the first four months of the current fiscal year. So an improvement in the fiscal situation looks very difficult, especially with tax revenues having risen only by 7 per cent as compared to this year's target growth of 17 per cent. But banks should be allowed to continue with 'lazy banking'. Many banks are holding SLRs in excess of stipulated requirements. Could they not be encouraged to withdraw the excess holdings and use it for meeting credit needs of the industry? RBI could change the ball game by reversing the SLR requirement and stipulating a maximum rather than a minimum holding of government securities. It will help achieve fiscal discipline as well.

Priority sector lending requirements imposed on commercial banks in some sense dilute their accountability and allow them to operate in sub-optimal manner. The Governor in his opening speech talked about the need "... to nudge banks into areas they would otherwise not venture into. But that mandate should adjust to the needs of the economy, and should be executed in the most efficient way possible." Economy's requirements have clearly changed and methods adopted by commercial banks to meet priority sector targets, may not necessarily be conducive to efficient banking. Why not simply do away with these requirements, which are more in the nature of being politically correct rather than serving any felt need. In any case, small and medium enterprises (SMEs) continue to be deprived of adequate commercial bank lending despite these priority sector requirements. So other effective ways have to be found to channel more credit in to the SMEs. Raghu will be interested to know that a recent survey showed that SMEs do not borrow from banks not because of the high rate of interest but because of the long and cumbersome procedures because of inordinately high collateral requirements that threaten to jeopardise the borrower's financial and livelihood security.

The appointment of a committee under Nachiket More for examining all aspects of financial inclusion is of course welcome. It would be better if the definition of financial inclusion could be clarified *ab initio*. For example it is difficult for some of us to accept that providing short term credit at interest rates of 20 per cent and above, qualifies as financial inclusion. And the committee would do well to examine how other countries achieve greater financial inclusion without taking recourse to self help groups (SHGs) and micro-credit agencies whose operations have justifiably come under sharp scrutiny and exposed as less than kosher. The question must be asked, if commercial banks, allowed the freedom to open their branches, liberated from priority sector lending and carrying a lower burden of holding government securities, cannot be the main instruments for financial inclusion. This question will become even more relevant if banks are allowed to collaborate with telecom service providers to spread mobile banking and make use of other IT enabled services.

Some issues, however, are still missing from the otherwise detailed first statement of intent by the Governor. I am sure he will come to these issues in due course. I refer to: the consolidation of public sector banks and privatising them after that; recalling RBI's representatives from the Boards of public sector banks even if the bank management offers reasonably sounding arguments in support of retaining them; allowing better performing NBFCs to graduate into specialised or sector specific banking companies under the 'on tap' licensing approach announced by the Governor; handling of the urban and rural credit cooperatives which fragment capacity and do not often adhere to prudential norms etc. These are important issues that have been ignored for far too long and require addressing, sooner rather than later.

Finally, the approach to monetary policy, it seems will become clear after three months when the committee headed by Urjit Patel puts in its recommendations. We need clarity on whether the RBI prefers monetary policy to be exclusively targeted on controlling inflation or will it continue to include growth and employment in its set of policy objectives. The RBI Act of 1934, cited by Raghu, is nicely vague as it asks the RBI to work "...with a view to securing monetary stability in India and generally to operate the currency and credit system of the country to its advantage." I am sure the investing community would like the RBI to be more explicit and that the RBI will include and assign some notional weights to the two other objectives of sustaining high rates of growth and expanding employment. In a developing economy these are key policy goals. In the interests of predictability and transparency (which the Governor has himself commended), the RBI should come out with a clear statement of the policy objectives it intends to pursue. It is a great start. As always there is far more to be done. Let us all give him the benefit of the doubt and hope he succeeds.

17

Time to Safeguard the Economy

I DO NOT RECALL any other Independence Day speech, in which the Prime Minister had to start not by one but two condolence messages. This is indeed unfortunate and sad for all of us but especially for the Prime Minister who was delivering his tenth and surely the last Independence Day address to the nation. This could have been his day if he had chosen to rise above partisan concerns and addressed his countrymen and women with the objective of arousing their flagging spirits and lift the dismal mood that envelops them. But most disappointingly Dr Manmohan Singh chose (he could not possibly have been following any instructions?) to use this very special occasion to read out, most un-inspiringly, a long list of his government achievements since 2004. In the midst of the prevailing doom and gloom and the foreboding sense of an even larger crisis in the offing, his was a tragic effort to hold a candle in the face of a storm. He and his advisors must have known that the litany of statistics, delivered in a deadpan fashion without any emotion could not even be the electoral bugle, which it was meant to be, let alone a stirring call to the ramparts to come together to save the economy from further damage.

As one of his most ardent well wisher and someone for whom Dr Manmohan Singh had been a role model since I worked under him in the early nineties, how I sincerely wish that he will now choose to step aside. He should let those who have constrained him beyond any reasonable limits handle the mess that we find ourselves in today. How long can he provide the cover for all the dishonesty and chicanery that has become the hallmark of our political process. In fact this might well be Dr Singh's 'lastest' chance to save some positive legacy as a prime minister. He should step aside, if not for his own sake, but for the sake of those who have looked up to him, admired his personal integrity and scholarship but who are today left feeling dejected and indeed embarrassed at the current anger that the people are displaying and not without reason. It is perhaps the first time in living memory that food inflation has been above 10 per cent continuously for the last 60 months—five years of inexorable rise in the cost of the consumption basket of the *aam aadmi*. The anger is therefore justified. The promise of rice at ₹3 per kilo is seen as an affront by our hard working people who do not want a life on permanent dole.

The tragic events of Uttarakhand and the loss of Sindhurakshak with her crew of 18 are not the only tragedies that have stuck the country in recent days. A greater tragedy, which could have been avoided, has been unfolding over the last two years. This has been the steady but sure loss of investors' confidence in the ruling dispensation. This is at the root of the economic downturn and the consequential external sector crisis that the government is desperately trying to manage with a slew of measures that are regressive and unfortunately unlikely to succeed.

The headlines on 67th Independence Day are about the re-imposition of capital controls on corporates and individuals with the objective of ring-fencing the Rupee and shore up its exchange rate. This has come along with the hike in import duties on bullion imports and administrative measures to curb the import of gold even by jewellers and exporters. These come on the heels of an earlier set of measures which failed to lift the Rupees exchange rate. I am left wondering how far is the government prepared to go with these 'band-aid' approach for addressing the serious external account crisis that we are now faced with. Will the next set of steps be restriction on current account transactions as well and an abrogation of our Article VIII commitments? Will the finance minister use the same argument as he has done for this round of capital controls that those who require the foreign exchange can get the necessary permission to do so from the RBI? Does that not pitch us right back to the pre-1991 days, hopefully temporarily? And will these administrative measures and higher duties on the bullion import not evoke exactly the same response of a spurt in *hawala* transactions and gold smuggling? The dhows in the middle-east and the *hundiwalas* of Mumbai, Chennai and Surat must all be sharpening their rusting instruments as we write this.

I am afraid the North Block is truly well behind the curve. We have to understand that increased gold imports reflect a capital flight and not a sudden rise in Indians' propensity for jewellery. And capital flight like a bank run, once it has started represents a loss of confidence that cannot be stopped by piecemeal measures. We need some real demonstration of Government's will to bite the bullet and take the right economic decisions, and not pander to electoral considerations by extolling the virtues of the food security bill, an unmitigated disaster in the making, from the ramparts of the red fort!

The market is in a punishing mood. The last announcement of the finance minister that he will restrict the current account deficit to $70 billion was greeted by the Rupee depreciating to 61.45 to one dollar. These new set of measures forcing the public sector enterprises to raise external borrowings and restricting capital outflows will in my view not comfort the market and not raise investors' confidence one bit. Instead they might well be seen as desperate measures by a government which will still not take the tough measures needed to raise investment.

It is time that the government admits to the severity of the crisis, sheds its electoral calculations and steps up to the plate to prevent the economy from plummeting into avoidable crisis. The first time the Congress left the economy in dire straits was in 1989 when the incoming government had to airlift the country's gold reserves to London. This time, with $170 billion worth of debt to be repaid in the next few months, we could again be in a most unenviable situation of lenders not willing to roll our debts. The UPA government owes it to the people of this country to ensure that such a contingency does not come to pass. For that to happen, band-aid measures will not suffice. The incoming RBI governor must know this and must force his former finance ministry colleagues to bite the bullet. If that implies approaching the IMF now rather than eight months later when the crisis has blown out of control, then that step, heart wrenching though it surely will be, must be taken now. Not a great way to celebrate independence but necessary to safeguard it.

18

LARR: A Mortal Blow for India's Modernisation

THE LAND ACQUISITION, Rehabilitation and Resettlement Bill, 2011 (LARR) is set to become law. Clearly, Indian farmers who pay zero taxes and contribute a mere 12 per cent of the GDP, command unquestioned loyalty of the political class. All other interests and national objectives are subservient to them. Our apprehension, shared by many others like Sanjoy Chakravorty's "On Land, No Lessons Learnt" carried by the Indian Express on August 30th, 2013 is that LARR, if made into law, will pretty much sound the death knell of industrialisation in India. With LARR in operation, the Commerce and Industry Minister has lost his battle and can just as well officially abandon the new manufacturing policy with its objective of increasing the manufacturing sector's share in GDP to 18 per cent. LARR will stop in its track the ambitious DMIC project and bring to a standstill the process of planned urbanisation in the country. In their populist frenzy, the political class, chasing electoral prospects, could be putting an end to all prospects of generating jobs in the industrial sector and permanently condemning the poor to live in slums. Let us explain.

The most damaging features of LARR are the extremely complicated procedures and provisions for any future land acquisition by the government for its own needs or for infrastructure projects to be undertaken via the PPP route. These procedures include: an open ended and complex social impact analysis for every acquisition; identifying those whose livelihoods will be affected and compensating them; sharing of capital gains with the original owner over the next 10 years; providing 25 different types of infrastructure services as part of the resettlement and rehabilitation (R&R) provisions;

prohibiting land acquisition beyond 5 per cent in districts with multi-crop agriculture and beyond 10 per cent in all single crop districts; requiring the approval of 80 per cent of land owners before acquisition can be completed; and authorising the district collector to arbitrarily determine the price of land rather than use a more objective basis for doing so. These complex procedures, put in place ostensibly to protect farmers' interests, will end up hurting them as the Bill will unleash a tsunami of red tape, litigation and administrative discretion rather than diminishing them as should have been its real objective. The industry and real estate sectors' demand for land will surely decline as PPP projects, which will face the complete uncertainty in land acquisition, come to a standstill. This is bound to result in decline in land prices that will hurt the landowners and trap them in their current low productivity operations.

Moreover, the entire panoply of LARR's R&R provisions apply with full force to private purchase of land (not acquisition by the government) if the size of the land being purchased is more than 100 acres in rural and more than 50 acres in urban areas. This is explicitly stated in Section 42 (clauses 1, 2, and 3) in Chapter VI which inter alia states that, "Where any person other than a specified person is purchasing land equal to or more than one hundred acres, in rural areas and fifty acres in urban areas, through private negotiations he shall file an application with the District Collector" who will " ...refer the matter to the Commissioner for the satisfaction of all relevant provisions under this Act related to rehabilitation and resettlement." And that each case will be individually examined. Therefore, all private purchases of land will be subject to administrative discretion and bear the substantial R&R costs. One can well imagine the extent of rent seeking, corruption and harassment that LARR will unleash when it becomes law. Have the BJP and other opposition parties actually understood these negative aspects of LARR while supporting the Bill?

The complicated procedures and processes enshrined in LARR are in themselves sufficient to derail all future industrial and urbanisation projects. However, these are further exacerbated by the huge increase in land costs as a consequence of LARR's pricing proposals, which could well make both industrial and housing projects simply unviable.

LARR proposes the following:

(i) Cost of land acquisition will be 4 times the market rate for rural land purchases and 2 times the market rate for urban purchases.

(ii) Land owner compensation will include: (a) ₹36,000 as one time allowance; (b) job for one family member, or ₹5,00,000 up front, or ₹24,000 per year, adjusted for inflation, for the next 20 years. Landowner will choose between the two remuneration policies; (c) ₹50,000 for transportation of landowner; (d) ₹50,000 for resettlement; (e) Buyer will construct a house if the landowner is being made to resettle; (f) If the land remains undeveloped, but appreciates in value, at time of resale, the original landowner will receive 20 per cent of the new value of the land;

(iii) Livelihood Loser Compensation (a person/family that generates its livelihood from the parcel of land in question and has been doing so for a minimum of three years). These families are distinct from landowners families) will include: (a) ₹36,000 one time allowance per family; (b) Job for one family member, or ₹5,00,000 up front, or ₹24,000 per year for the next 20 years; (c) ₹50,000 for transportation; (d) ₹50,000 for resettlement.

(iv) In case any of the two categories are part of the SC/ST section, they will receive an additional: (a) 2.5 acres of land; (b) Additional allowance of ₹50,000; and (c) Space for gathering, meeting and community. (It should be clarified that this pricing formulae applies only to acquired land and not to privately purchase of land for which only the R&R provisions are applicable.)

On the basis of the above provisions and assuming that there is single owner of land and five families have earned their livelihood from each acre of land, the increase in price of land in five different locations in the country will be as follows:

Area	*State*	*Current Rate per Acre (₹)**	*LARR Rate per Acre (₹)*	*Landowner Compensation (₹)*	*Livelihood Compensation (₹)*	*Total Cost per Acre (₹)*
Anand Bhandhani CLhokadi	Gujarat	1,52,46,000	6,09,84,000	6,36,000	31,80,000	6,48,00,000
Nayi Basti Maanpur	Uttarakhand	30,71,673	1,22,86,692	6,36,000	31,80,000	1,61,02,692
Nasrullganj	Madhya Pradesh	12,90,993	51,63,972	6,36,000	31,80,000	89,79,972
Kinathukadavu	Tamil Nadu	61,43,346	2,45,73,384	6,36,000	31,80,000	2,83,89,384
Bhahadurgarh	Punjab	3,57,47,151	14,29,88,604	6,36,000	31,80,000	14,68,04,604

Note: * Prices taken as listed on *99acres.com*, a real estate search portal. These are asking prices, converted from square meter to acre in some cases.

The costs of R&R provision, detailed above and in addition, the costs of providing 25 infrastructure services, (spelled out in paragraph 17 of the Statement of Objects and Reasons) have to be added to the above price. The services to be included will add substantially to the price as these include: schools and play grounds, health centres, roads and electricconnections, assured sources of safe drinking water, panchayat ghars, Anganwadis, places of worship, burial and cremation grounds, village level post offices, fair price shops and seed-cum-fertilisers storage facilities!! It is not unreasonable to estimate that a minimum of ₹1 crore per acre would be added to the price of land on account of R&R and infrastructure services. On average, therefore, the price of land in rural areas will increase five times with LARR coming in to force. LARR will make land far more expensive and make it subject to complex procedures and non-transparent administrative discretion.

Price of acquiring rural land in India will, according to the above table, range between $138,000 per acre (Nasrulganj, Madhya Pradesh) to $2.25 million per acre (Bhahadurgarh, Punjab). This compares to $2,140 per acre in the US at current prices and $19,595 per acre in France.[1] India's competing countries in Asia will have land cost at a fraction of these prices and also active government support in acquiring them without the long procedural hassles. Is there any reason to believe that foreign or domestic investors will consider putting up manufacturing capacities under these conditions. If we assume that for putting up a 100 MW thermal power plant, an investor would require 50 acres of rural land. According to the above table, it would imply a land cost of between ₹50 crore to ₹700 crore. With total fixed costs estimated at ₹6 crore per MW, these land costs amount to between 9 to a whopping 110 per cent of total costs of putting up a thermal power plant. This will apply equally to all other manufacturing sectors and real estate projects. In the case of low cost housing for the poor, the hike in land costs will make these projects completely unviable.

---

1. Financial Times, "European Farmland Hits Record Prices". *http://www.ft.com/intl/cms/s/0/55c8dc0c-1159-11dd-a93b-0000779fd2ac.html#axzz1SPcHftLI*

With these features, LARR could conceivably result in India's de-industrialisation in the coming years. Its negative impact will also be felt by the farmers who will now be unable to move out of low productivity agriculture operations. The poor will suffer as well as they will not be able to afford proper housing. This cannot possibly be the objective of the political class in passing this Bill. As this article argues, the opposition parties can build a strong case for opposing the Bill on grounds that it will vitally affect the interests of those it seeks to support and in addition will result in a sharp decline in manufacturing activity in India. Surely we need to rethink before it is too late.

19

Push Back the Luddites

THE LUDDITES have won for the moment. A mere 10 million owners of traditional and self-organised retail and wholesale trade have held the country of 1.2 billion people to ransom and thwarted progress. Their pyrrhic victory has been achieved by evoking the fear of 40 million people associated with the sector being thrown out of jobs and livelihood. This is gross misrepresentation of facts. It is yet another demonstration (like central planning is more efficient than a regulated market) of how untruth can triumph when repeated often and loudly enough. The retail sector is destined to almost double in size in the next 10 years by simply keeping pace with growth. By 2022, the size of the unorganised retail sector is estimated to reach nearly $1,000 billion. Of this, the 'mom and pop stores' are expected to have a market share of 84 per cent, giving them a business volume of $840 billion—a huge expansion from their current market of $450 billion! Can anyone, who is opposing the entry of FDI in retail trade and thereby preventing the modernisation of the sector please explain how an expansion in business from $450 to more than $800 billion will result in the death, demise, destitution and deprivation of this most resilient and intrepid group of traders? Munshi Premchand, the doyen amongst Hindi writers, who so eloquently described the exploitative and ruthless ways of this class, must surely be turning in his grave at seeing this travesty of the trader receiving the support and sympathy of political leaders who are ostensibly wedded to the welfare of the 'aam aadmi'. A greater irony could not be visualised and can come about only in our country where competitive populism seems to have trumped any rational discourse.

The other fear that has been purposely spread is that this step will take India back to becoming a colony of foreign powers. This is done by resurrecting the ghost of the British East India Company that entered India in 1612 by asking for a trading concession from emperor

Jehangir. The rest as they say is colonial history. Are those evoking this fear serious in arguing that India in 2011 is as vulnerable, divided, weak and inept as it was four centuries ago?! If they truly believe this, both their integrity and nationalism must be thoroughly examined. India, today is at the cusp of attaining global power recognition. It is actively striving for and being supported by others for a permanent seat in the UN Security Council. A large number of developing and emerging economies look towards India as a model for their own development. And in complete contrast to all this positive sentiment about our great country, some amongst would have us believe that a bunch of foreign retail stores, selling food, toiletries and assorted merchandise can outwit, outthink and outgun the country's leadership and elite. This reflects a very low opinion of our abilities and indeed very poor self-esteem. Can a country whose people have such a poor opinion of themselves really rise to assume global responsibilities? Can my friends in the BJP, avowedly a party with strong nationalist sentiments, not see the stark contradiction in this fear of the foreigner and their exemplary nationalism? We have to show to the world and more importantly prove to ourselves that we can determine our own destiny. This is to be achieved not by denying ourselves the progress that is possible by working with foreign investors but by acting sagaciously, with foresight and resolve, if foreign investors diverge from our national priorities.

I daresay that those who have opposed the entry of FDI in multi-brand retail, have done this without recognising that this is a sector that remains backward, dominated by a cash economy with all its features of non-accountability and has poor to horrible working conditions. The same class of traders, which is being pampered with all the political attention today, does not even blink an eyelid in cutting regulatory corners and flouting all rules and regulations of which there is a plethora weighing on them. These are meant largely to be ignored and used predominantly for generating rent for the army of inspectors. Perhaps these features of the unorganised retail trade makes it attractive to those who would rather let our economy run on cash and keep our young people trapped in low productivity and insecure jobs. It is indeed a real pity that all our otherwise active civil society and consumer welfare organisations choose to ignore the poor working conditions and anti-consumer welfare aspects of the unorganised retail sector. This is as hypocritic as accepting child labour as domestic help while protesting loudly for the right to children education and against child labour otherwise. It is also a pity that farmers' organisations have not come out more strongly in favour of large scale organised retail trade which will give them higher returns, better terms of trade and even access to better farming practices. The lesson from this unfortunate episode is that it is important for those who are advocating reforms for greater liberalisation and globalisation to also better organise themselves and take the trouble to present their case to the public. The setback to bringing in the FDI in retail trade demonstrates unambiguously and strongly that reforms can never be undertaken by stealth. A public case has to be built and propagated strongly to push back the Luddites.

20

Making a Win-Win Non-Populist Budget

THE ANNUAL PRE-BUDGET economists' meeting with the finance minister and his team was held on 7th January. It is quite amazing how such practices tend to get a life of their own, even if over the years their utility is not clearly visible. I sincerely believe that much better purpose would be served if these pre-budget meetings were held at the beginning of October, which is the start of the budget making process. That would give time for the suggestions to be worked out in the relevant departments and another round of consultations where required. Also, it may be worthwhile for the Government to put forward some of its own ideas for feedback from participants. This will help to change the present nature of these meetings where invariably one side submits and the other side stoically listens. That is hardly a recipe for constructive participation!

As expected, the economists threw up a rich and wide ranging fare for the finance minister's consideration. On some issues, however, there was a near consensus—quite an achievement for ten economists, 'present and speaking' (with due apologies to those present and do not agree with my interpretation). There was a consensus that the finance minister is in an unviable position and has a very hard act to perform. Given the acute need for restoring fiscal balance, necessary to shore up investor sentiment, he cannot afford to be even perceived let alone be populist in the forthcoming budget. But we know that he will be under tremendous pressure to announce freebies and handouts in this last budget before the next general election. On the last occasion, in February 2008, he had delivered handsomely by increasing public expenditure by as much as 3.5 per cent of GDP for financing the farm loan waiver, huge expansion in MNREGA allocations and generous increases for social sector spending. But on this occasion he unfortunately does not have the luxury of a booming economy. He has to find the additional revenues before he can plan his outlays with an eye on electoral prospects.

There was also consensus against the idea of introducing a higher tax bracket for the super rich. Several economists felt that the proposal floated by the Chairman of the PMEAC was ill-timed. Such a move will 'spook the market' and vitiate the investment sentiment at a time when the need of the hour was to strengthen the investment cycle. Tax evasion and generation of black money will also increase. Moreover, there was a widespread feeling that far more efforts could be made to widen the tax net and improve compliance. I pointed out that there are nearly 125 million non-agriculture households in the country. Of these we can assume that 40 million are below the poverty line and another 20 million households or 16 per cent would be below the exemption limit. At present there are only 36 million taxpayers in the country. However, even assuming that each taxpayer represented a single household, it still leaves nearly 30 million which could and should be brought within the tax net. We should also note that only 40 per cent of rural households earn more than 50 per cent of their income from agriculture. So some of the 125 million agriculture households should also be brought into the tax net. This will nearly double the revenues from personal income tax and also be more fair and equitable for the honest tax payers. Why is this not possible?

It is also a well known fact that only 1.4 million tax payers declare their annual income to be above ₹10 million, which is a travesty. We know that there are legions of doctors, lawyers, chartered accountants, traders, real estate agents and share brokers, architects, private tutors, other self-employed who would be earning higher amounts. Unfortunately, there seemed to be a degree of helplessness, indeed defeatism, about preventing under-declaration of incomes by the dishonest citizen. We could learn from other jurisdictions on making income tax officials more adept and honest at identifying the true number of high income earners. Governance in this most important department must improve. Perhaps honouring our honest revenue officers with national recognition along with handsome cash awards can be the first step. I know of so many honest revenue officers who received nothing extra, for their honesty and integrity and many who were harassed and transferred while doing an honest job. The working ethos and practices in our revenue departments both at the central and state levels must change. Increasing the revenue from direct taxes will have the double benefit of reducing the generation of black money and allowing a reduction in indirect taxes that bring down prices and expand demand.

There is also a very strong case for higher efficiency of public expenditures. In one of his previous stints as finance minister, Mr Chidambaram had introduced the important concepts of zero budgeting and outcome based budgets. But as with many other good ideas, these have withered for want of necessary support in an environment of bureaucratic inertia and political neglect. It is time to implement these initiatives as a sustained determined effort. There are so many government agencies, which we know, do not add value. Such 'non-jobs' also demoralise honest officers. Along with rationalising the plethora of centrally sponsored schemes, it is time to take the axe to these agencies, departments, institutes and corporations that serve no ostensible purpose. 23 of the 51 ministries have spent less than 50 per cent of their budgeted outlays in eight months (April-November) and 31 have spent less than 60 per cent. They should not be allowed to splurge in the last quarter as this encourages wasteful and unaccountable expenditure. This is the time to demonstrate to the electorate that the government is serious in getting greater bang for the tax payers buck. This will be a real incentive for better compliance.

21

Food Security Bill Will Hurt not Help the Poor in India

THE CHIEF SPOKESPERSON of the Congress party, Mr Ajay Maken in a live television interview, apparently took great pride in reeling out that in 2004, the food subsidy bill was only ₹25,000 crore (about $4.5 billion), which will rise to a massive ₹1.25 lakh crore (about $23 billion) by the time the Food Security Bill (FSB) that his party is pushing through a Presidential ordinance, is implemented. He was very clearly claiming that by increasing the food subsidy bill five times, his party had proven its pro-poor credentials! The needle has turned full circle. In Indian politics, we now brag about our fiscal profligacy and not try to hide it. This degree of brazenness must leave us aghast. But the question to ask is whether the FSB will actually help the poor or would they in fact be worse off in the coming period as a result of this measure.

Common knowledge tells us that Indians are presently not starving and there are no reports, not even from the most backward districts of food deprivation and hunger deaths. Yes there is deprivation but this is surely due to a shortage of proteins, vegetables, fruits and poultry products, that are priced out of the reach of the poor. It is surely not a result of the poor being unable to access basic food grains in any part of our country. If that was the case, our political leaders would have faced the wrath of the people much earlier for allowing millions of tonnes of food grain to rot in Food Corporation of India (FCI) storage as happens with pathetic regularity. With assured returns from even higher procurement by the FCI, farmers will be even more dis-incentivised to produce any other product except food grains. The existing distortion in supply response in the agriculture sector will get even worse and the food price inflation for non-food grain commodities, which are in higher demand will be aggravated. The result will be that the poor who are deprived of these necessary nutrients will be further pushed out and suffer even more food related deprivation as a consequence of the FSB.

But this is certainly not the entire negative impact. All those who propagate the FSB know as well, that the poorest in India are effectively excluded from the coverage of the public distribution system (PDS). The large majority of the actual poor have to fend for themselves in the open market. Migrant workers on all construction sites, hawkers, rickshaw pullers etc., are just not covered by the government's corruption ridden and highly leaky PDS, which remains highly biased towards the formal sector. These really poor people, who have to depend on the market for their daily dietary needs, will face higher prices even for food grains as a result of the FSB. This will be a direct consequence of higher procurement by the FCI. Thus, the residual supplies reaching the open markets will be much smaller, forcing up the food grain prices and in all likelihood also resulting in shortages and supply bottlenecks. The poor will face even greater hardships as the cost of basic necessities rises even higher. And yet the Congress party will hit the electoral road claiming that they have worked for the poor's welfare.

I am, therefore dumbfounded that all this is happening under the watch of Dr Manmohan Singh, Mr Montek S Ahluwalia, Dr C. Rangarajan and Dr Raghuram Rajan, who was the chief economist of the IMF, an agency that stood for (am not sure now) for fiscal rectitude and prudence. I do not include the finance minister Mr P. Chidambaram, because being a quintessential politician of the highest calibre, he has played the game earlier. In the February 2008 budget, he let public expenditure expand by a full 3.5 per cent points of the GDP. I have since maintained that we Indians are so clever that our leaders anticipated the Lehman crisis and reflated ahead of it! That successfully paved the way for UPA's electoral triumph in May 2009. But we are still paying the price of fiscal indiscipline that led the way to good economic policy being completely sacrificed to political expediency in the first three years of UPA II, and which has seen the economy turn turtle with lowest GDP growth rates in more than 10 years. During 1991-1995, when I had worked in the Ministry of Finance, headed by Dr Singh and Mr Ahluwalia, they would not tire of warning us against the dangers of competitive populism and fiscal recklessness. No less than the government's own chief agriculture economist, Dr Ashok Gulati, the chairman of Commission of Agriculture Costs and Prices (CACP) has repeatedly warned of the unsustainable fiscal burden that this one act will put on the public fisc. But alas to no avail. However, I want to emphasise that it is not the fiscal un-sustainability but the negative impact on the poor that should force a re-think by all concerned on going ahead with the FSB.

FSB allows this government to proudly claim that they have made food security a right that can be legally enforced. The irony is supreme. Can we seriously argue that the poor will actually move to legally enforce their right to sufficient food!! Has the Right to Education seen legal action to take children off the streets and away from horrible work places? Has the Right to Information made governance transparent and not full of unprecedented scams and crony capitalism? This populist trend to legislate economic rights without due attention to providing gainful employment is populism run amuck. It should leave us dumbfounded because all this is being overseen by avowedly the 'best economists.'

The Congress Party legalises the right to food while at the same time overseeing economic growth rate decline to 4.8 per cent from the 8.5 per cent it had inherited in 2004. It has allowed private investment to come to a near complete stop and seen private capital outflows from India become larger than inflows. Industrial sector growth has plummeted from more than 10 per cent to less than 2 per cent now and soon enough firms will be laying off workers. New employment opportunities have practically dried up already. Clearly, the ruling party thinks that there is no contradiction between its promise of food security and greater unemployment. They perhaps forget that after nearly 15 years of sustained growth, even the poorest Indians are more concerned about a dignified existence that comes from being gainfully employed and not interested in living on charity or dole. Our leaders must realise that India today needs to create 1 million new jobs every month (yes 12 million every year) for the next 10 years or longer to simply absorb the entrants to the workforce. As jobs dry up, these youngsters will become gun fodder to expanding groups of extremists and fundamentalists. A terrifying prospect and a certain path to social and economic ruination that the country can ill afford.

22

Sonawane's Sacrifice

Subsidies Sans Rationale

SONWANE'S RECENT HORRIFIC and brazen murder by the kerosene mafia in Maharashtra has left us numbed and in a state of despair. This was not the first murder related to the dysfunctional system of kerosene subsidy that all our senior policy makers know is a ₹10, 000 crore scam perpetrated, year after year, in the name of the poor. Unfortunately, in our country, public memories, in these days of bytes and 24x7 sensationalism, are terribly short. Hardly any print or electronic media connected Sonawane being burnt alive to the daylight murder a young IOC engineer in the prime of his life by the same kerosene mafia in Lalu's Bihar. Manjunath, like Sonwane had made the fatal mistake of trying to prevent wholesale leakage of kerosene from IOC depots. Our governance systems no more protect the honest. Alarming is it not!

The more disturbing feature of these subsidy related murders is the predictable official response. In both cases there was an expected flurry of official activity with some arrests of known criminals, official pronouncements for zero tolerance for corruption and promises to end the leakage. Fat chance. And yes within a week of the horrific incidents officials slipped back into their humdrum but important businesses of representations, delegations, convocations and felicitations. The media too, driven mercilessly by TRP ratings, conveniently switched to the next attention grabbing story which as bizarre irony coming so soon after Sonwane's subsidy provoked murder, dealt with incredible India showing off its resilience at the Adda in Davos! Unfortunately, Sonawane and Manjunath are not Jessica Lal and murders committed by the mafia of honest, upright and brave public officials have no glamorous quotient to be exploited. And discretion demands that one can take on a lone deviant politician but better not to pursue an entrenched mafia with its money backed nexus with the ruling establishments.

Is it not time to get away from the mere symptoms and try and plug the financial flows that nurture these criminal networks that are spreading criminality in our social fabric? First let us debunk the myth that such activity can be stopped by administrative actions. Well meaning leftist friends must recognise that given our national realities, even the proletariat government in West Bengal with an unbroken rule of more than three decades has not been successful in ensuring that public subsidies flow to targeted beneficiaries. All the awards for good performance and fanfare accompanying them, cannot hide the fact that even under MGNREGA, by far the most closely monitored subsidy scheme, huge amounts of resources are usurped by the intermediaries. There is another kind of network and nexus at work here which benefits the middle level political agents in collusion with the local officials with the active connivance of their seniors. As an extreme irony, Sonawane's ultimate sacrifice, coming right in the midst of budget making could not be better timed. It should have sent a galling reminder to all concerned that it is time to try and wash away the bloodstains from this dysfunctional system of subsidies by closing the spout and redirecting the resources to actually help the poor. I am reminded of the early nineties, when policy makers were actually undertaking reforms rather than only professing and proclaimng their benefits, when in order to stop the mafia activities arising from bullion smuggling, the simple but far reaching measure of legalising allowing gold imports at a nominal custom duty was implemented. Haji Mastan's (remember him?) empire collapsed in no time.

So for us who will like these murders to not continue, the far reaching and most effective measure that could be announced in the forthcoming budget would be to abolish the kerosene subsidy. To reiterate, everyone knows that it only benefits those who use it for adulteration of petrol and diesel and does not reach the poor. Is it not extreme dishonesty and callousness to not stop this huge drain on the public exchequer in the name of the *aam admi* to feed the corrupt and murderous criminal gangs? Will this happen only after the judiciary intervenes and takes up this case *suo moto* and asks to be given an estimate of the percentage of this subsidy that actually reaches the poor? Has there ever been even at attempt to evaluate the effectiveness of this subsidy?

Lest I be charged of speaking against the interests of the poor, being stereotyped as a representative of big business, let me suggest that this amount of ₹10,000 crore will be far better utilised as scholarship money for poor students. I am an actual beneficiary of the government scholarship system having received my first scholarship at the age of twelve that propelled me from a rote shop in Lucknow to a well endowed public school in Delhi. So I know it works. Given the times and the governance breakdown, the critical feature however would be to allocate ₹9,800 crore for scholarships and ₹200 crore for the scheme's implementation by a private agency that is regulated directly by the CAG. Perhaps expand the budget allocation for the National Skill Development Corporation (NSDC) which can implement the scheme. The poor will be benefitted far more by this measure and the Maharashtra government will not have to waste time and resources going after the kerosene mafia. It will collapse overnight.

23

Creating New Entitlements

The Wrong Way to Achieve Food Security

THE PARLIAMENTARY Standing Committee on Food has made some new recommendations that in effect lower the coverage to 67 per cent of the total population and reduces the entitlement to five kilograms of food grains per person. My friends on the left have consistently argued for universal coverage for subsidised food on the rather spurious basis that any selection is fraught with malpractices and so carries serious risk of leaving out the real beneficiaries. This is indeed ironical because, while being convinced of the governance weaknesses that precludes a proper identification of beneficiaries, leftists are strangely convinced that the public sector will be able to handle this gigantic task of handling the procurement, storage, transportation and delivery of about 50 million tonnes food grains each year, needed to provide subsidised food for 167.5 million households that will be entitled for coverage in 2013. To achieve this, the Food Corporation of India (FCI) will have to expand its capacity pretty much overnight by a whopping 40 per cent. The quantum of food grains required will only increase inexorably until at least 2035 when the population is expected to stabilise at 1.6 billion. The extent of FCI's inefficiency is well known. As an example, presently it has storage capacity of 36 million tonnes to cater to a stock on 66 million tonnes as on 1 November 2012! I wonder at the reasons due to which the entire political class, which supports the Food Security Bill (FSB), is shutting its eyes to the massive potential waste and leakage, which is inevitable in such a massive expansion in the public distribution system (PDS).

There is then also the fiscal burden of the proposed Bill, which has been so forcefully and repeatedly pointed out by none other than Dr Ashok Gulati, Chairman of the Commission on Agriculture Costs and Prices (CACP). This bears no repetition. With economic costs of wheat and rice being officially given as ₹18.22 and ₹24. 2 per kilogram, (*Food Grain Bulletin*, Ministry of Consumer Welfare) the average subsidy per kilogram works out to ₹16 for wheat and ₹21 for rice. This will be even higher in the years in which food grains may have to be imported. Is this level of subsidy conceivably sustainable? No amount of increase in tax rates or widening of the direct tax net can possibly fill this fiscal hole. Therefore, any attempt to use the marginal fiscal space created by raising diesel and petroleum prices for funding the huge outlay for the FSB will be seen as a serious compromise in maintaining the promised fiscal balance and may result in a costly downgrade by credit agencies. More importantly perhaps it will be seen as succumbing once again to populist pressures in the face of an impending election, despite the clear knowledge that it can potentially derail the economy.

Supporters of the Bill argue that putting two square meals each day on a poor family's table is the best way of empowering them and that this cannot be shelved any longer. Nobody can argue against ensuring food security for all Indians. The issue is if this can be met more effectively by lowering relative prices of food grains and other agriculture products along with raising the purchasing power of the poor by giving them good quality employment. This is far superior to making the poor dependent on a hugely inefficient, wasteful and corruption ridden food grain PDS that will only prolong their vulnerability.

Moreover, is it the case that 67 per cent of our population is actually poor and needs statutory assurance for receiving subsidised food grains? Perhaps, the existence of huge food grain stocks reveals that India has already achieved reasonable food security for its people. Yet it is true that nearly half of our children are undernourished. Would it not be therefore more humane, more welfare enhancing and socially more justifiable to target additional outlays on getting greater nutrition for the children rather than spend them on this catch all Ferny entitlement, which includes the non-deserving and will substantially increase corruption and leakages in the system.

We should use our public sector outlays to empower our people in a real sense. This would not be achieved by creating a series of statutory entitlements that remain largely on paper and like the right to education, cannot be implemented. Instead of frittering away our revenues on putting in place a leaky, wasteful and unsustainable Food Security Act, political leadership of all parties should seriously consider using public expenditure to finance a very large system of education scholarships, a set of public and government banks, and in improving the public health system. This will create the necessary skills, reduce the risk of slipping into poverty due to illness and be far more effective in empowering the people than enacting the FSB.

It is a pity that none of the political parties have dared to oppose the bill except for the left which wants it to have even a wider coverage and lower prices! The consequences of the Act on the entire network of private food grain traders and transporters will be most disruptive. This would be similar to the widespread disruption and disaffection that gripped the county after the wheat trade was nationalised in 1974. It is therefore important that leadership across the political spectrum sees the ominous writings on the wall and persuades the government to shelve the Bill. The opposition will do itself and the government and the country a big favour by behaving less opportunistically and forcing the government to adhere to the targets laid down by the FRBM Act.

24

Food Security Bill

Its Hidden Costs and Consequences

THE FOOD SECURITY BILL (FSB) is fait accompli. The UPA, now desperate to pull some rabbits out of the hat to maximise its electoral prospects, did not want to take the risk of facing the parliament and has used the ordinance route. Not that any political party would have opposed such a populist measure and face the consequences of being called 'anti-people.' I have argued earlier that the FSB with its exclusive focus on food grain/cereal availability may well end up hurting the poor on two major counts. It will discourage the needed diversification in agriculture and aggravate the shortages of proteins, dairy, fruits and vegetables, whose consumption will redress malnourishment, which is the real problem that we face today. Secondly, the huge increase in centralised procurement of food grains will end up raising their market prices and the real poor, who remains outside the coverage of the leaky public distribution system (PDS) system, will suffer the consequences. A more careful reading of the Act, reveals other costs that will ultimately have to be borne by the *aam aadmi* and which therefore need to be spelled out to recognise the actual deleterious consequences of this measure.

The proponents of the FSB like Jean Drèze are too facile in dismissing the concerns about the fiscal burden of the FSB as being 'wildly exaggerated'. But the fact is that the costs of implementing the Act are truly staggering. Gulati *et al.* (2012)[1] have estimated after detailed and meticulous calculations, that have not been challenged by any of the FSB supporters, the cost of implementing the Act in its first year as

1. Gulati, Ashok, Jyoti Gujral, T. Nand Kumar, Surbhi Jain, Sourabh Anand, Siddharth Rath and Piyush Joshi (2012). "National Food Security Bill, Challenges and Options", *Discussion paper* No.2. New Delhi: Commission on Agriculture Costs and Prices.

₹2.4 lakh crore which declines but only marginally to ₹2.2 lakh crore in the third year. Kumar and Ghosh (2012;[2] 2012a[3]) made a more conservative estimate, which did not include the infrastructure and logistics costs of implementing the Act and still came up with estimates of ₹1.43 lakh crore in the first year rising to ₹1.62 lakh crore in the third year. To say that the FSB is simply a re-structuring of existing PDS schemes and will not raise the fiscal burden is simply being disingenuous.

These are huge magnitudes amounting to 1.5 per cent of the GDP at the minimum and 2.4 per cent of the GDP at the higher end. This will double the total subsidy bill and put extraordinary pressure on the fiscal balance. There are multiple costs of this fiscal profligacy for the poor. They will suffer from inflation, which will be a necessary consequence of fiscal expansion and the attendant leakages which are estimated to be at least 40 per cent of the total bill. Second, in an attempt to keep the fiscal deficit within the target in the budget and yet make room for the additional outlays on the FSB, severe cuts have been imposed on expenditures in other ministries and departments. These are slowing down infrastructure projects and in fact even hurting the banking sector as several large borrowers are unable to service their loans due to slower progress of their projects and payments being held up. The poor are the worst affected by the infrastructure deficit as they do not have the means to find private solutions due to lack of necessary public services. Third, with the government borrowing more from the market, the upward pressure on market interest remains high and prevents capital costs from coming down. The consequence is continued investment drought resulting in a further slowdown of economic growth and drying up of employment opportunities. Here too the worst affected will be the poor.

Section 21 of the Act provides for the creation of new position of District Grievance Redressal Officer in each district. Section 22 requires State Governments to establish a State Food Commission

2. Kumar, Rajiv and Soumya Kanti Ghosh (2012). "Subsidy: It Will Not Stop at ₹60,000 Crore", *Indian Express*, 15 February.

3. ———. (2012a). "Last Straw on the Fisc Back", *Indian Express*, 16 February.

with a Chairman and five other members and a member secretary of the rank of a joint secretary to service the Commission. And best of all, Section 37 mandates the setting up of Vigilance Committees (composition and numerical strength unspecified) at the state, district, block and fair price shop levels. I tried to estimate the total number of new government jobs that will be created as a result of these provisions but failed when it came to the Vigilance Committees!! For a government so badly strapped for cash that it is substantively cutting down the country's defence outlay, this is indeed an inexcusable splurge of public money on creating of hundreds if not thousands of new positions in the government and for vaguely defined roles and accountability.

There is, however, one rather inexplicable provision in the Act which may nullify all its good intentions. This comes at the very end in Section 52, which provides an amazing caveat in its implementation. The section reads, "The Central Government, or as the case may be, the State Government, shall be liable for a claim by any person entitled under this Act, *except* (emphasis mine) *in the case of war, floods, drought, fire, cyclone or earthquake* affecting the regular supply of food grains or meals to such persons under the Act." This is an amazing provision because it implies that the Act will not be operational in any emergency when the potential beneficiaries are most vulnerable and require the greatest help. In short it implies that under the Act those affected by the cloudburst and its horrific aftermath in Uttarakhand cannot claim their entitlement of food under the Act!! Do we seriously need such a deeply flawed Act and push it through an ordinance? Specially one which has the potential to wreck the country's fiscal balance, slowdown the economy and result in severe distortions in both production and marketing of agriculture output. One hopes the political class will still pull back from the precipice.

25

Conditional Cash Transfers

The Time is Now

FISCAL SUBSIDIES FOR the middle class are here to stay. None of the political parties have mentioned any reduction let alone elimination of subsidies in their manifestoes for the ongoing parliamentary elections. One can only hope that some parties and especially the BJP, if it come to power, will not feel bound by their manifestoes and move to do away with atleast those subsidies which can be seen to be dysfunctional and which do not reach the intended beneficiaries. One such is the kerosene subsidy. From several studies and anecdotal evidence it is clear that a major chunk of the kerosene subsidy is misused for adulteration of petrol with kerosene. Officers who tried to stop this nefarious practice have had to pay with their lives. Similarly, the fertiliser subsidy does not go directly to the farmers who use them but to the producers, some of whom can continue with their outdated manufacturing capacities rather be forced to modernise them. Consequently, fertiliser subsidies perpetuate inefficiency and high costs, which in turn raise the cost of producing food grains and stoking inflation. Therefore, the first best outcome would still be for the incoming government to do away with these subsidies that encourage wasteful consumption, degradation of our natural resources and industrial inefficiency. Such bold steps will have to be taken in the first few months of taking office so that the positive consequences of curbing fiscal profligacy and switching to market determined prices can emerge well before the opposition can be mobilised and people get sucked into a costly strife and agitation against doing away with the subsidies.

But we have to be prepared that such an outcome is highly unlikely. Going by their manifestoes, political parties do not appear to have the necessary will to alienate the middle class which is undoubtedly the principal beneficiary of these subsidies though they are marketed as being intended for the poor. In this situation, it may be useful to consider some alternatives for a more efficient delivery of these subsidies to the intended beneficiaries. An oft discussed option is to monetise the value of all the subsidies that are received by an individual or a household and transfer the amount directly to his bank account. This form of cash transfer, in lieu of product specific subsidies, is seen to be less distortionary and also more efficient as it has far less avenues for leakages and misappropriation. Additionally, as in Brazil, such cash transfers can be made conditional on the beneficiary achieving some stipulated goals like keeping the girl child in school or immunising the children against specific diseases etc. Conditional cash transfers are now seen to be the more efficient, effective and least distortionary means of affording higher consumption for the poorer segments of the population. The resistance against it comes expectedly from the middle class beneficiaries who face near certain exclusion from such a scheme as they will not be eligible on any reasonable income criteria.

Conditional cash transfers can be implemented only and only if there is a foolproof and well developed method of identifying the targeted beneficiaries. Universalisation of the Aadhar Card promised to offer the solution to this vexed problem as it provided a relatively foolproof method of biometric identification that could be digitally connected across multiple dimensions of an individual's (or households) economic activities. Just like the social security number in the US and other advanced economies, Aadhar has the potential to inter-connect the beneficiary's bank account, income source, family information with details of ongoing schooling and health status. This can be very useful in ensuring the desired compliance of conditions stipulated for the cash transfer. Making Aadhar mandatory for receiving the subsidy amount and also using it for other economic activities like opening a bank account or admitting a child in school could provide the needed platform for operationalising the conditional cash transfers in place of the present set of product specific subsidies.

It would be far more arduous and complicated (of course not impossible) to implement the conditional cash transfer scheme in the absence of a versatile identification mechanism like the Aadhar card. Therefore, the incoming government should very carefully consider any suggestion to do away with the Aadhar card. Not only will such a move destroy a vast and carefully constructed programme which has used nearly a thousand crore of taxpayers' money, but it will also stymie any move to shift away from the present system of subsidies to the more robust and efficient 'conditional cash transfers' as the principal modality for welfare payments. Aadhar also offers the possibility, if implemented with due care and under even more effective supervision to root out some malpractices that have reportedly crept in inevitably, to weed out the fake identity cards and eliminate ghost beneficiaries from the system.

The major criticism of Aadhar, valid to an extent, is that it offers citizenship to its holders without adequate due diligence. Anybody residing in India with the required number of proof of residence can acquire an Aadhar card even if he or she may not qualify to be an Indian citizen. This is perhaps a major lacuna in the system and it is rather surprising that this was not spotted earlier and rectified. The reason could well be the tussle over turf between the Aadhar administration and the Ministry of Home Affairs that has been preparing the National Population Register (NPR) and sees itself as the exclusive authority for adjudicating on an individual's right to be an Indian citizen. My suggestion would be for the new government to resolve this rather petty turf war and require all Aadhar card holders to also declare their place and date of birth as a necessary condition for obtaining the Aadhar cards. Only those who are born in the country would be given the Aadhar card. This would ensure that the card is not misused for claiming Indian citizenship. For those who have already acquired these cards, a special programme could be launched to collect this information and required action be taken. There may well be some better ways to get over this problem. The government could also appoint a small group to examine if Aadhar suffers from other weaknesses and suggest means to overcome them. A way forward for achieving greater convergence between the national identity card and Aadhar and a level of synergy between the two departments could also be suggested. It will be indeed a pity to dismantle the entire platform that has been put in place over the past five years. Aadhar also offers a good example of a high level of efficiency in the public sector and can serve as a model for expanding e-governance to other government departments as well, especially those which are responsible for delivery of public services and collection of vital statistics. The government could consider using the same system for collecting much needed data on health and employment indicators that are inadequately available at present. It is surely more efficient to redesign and improve an existing platform and putting it to better use rather than junking it in a hurry.

26

Building Indigenous Think Tanks

THE INDIAN RULING establishment wants India to be a leader in global knowledge economy. Saudi Arabia has more limited aspiration of building world class research capacity in energy related fields. But it backs up its aspirations, by setting up a world class think tank, the King Abdullah Petroleum Research and Studies Centre. KAPSARC has been given an initial endowment of (hold your breath) $4 billion, which is estimated to grow to $20 billion over the next 25 years. On a conservative basis, this will allow KAPSARC a current annual revenue expenditure of $200 million. A separate allocation has been made for the capital expenditure for necessary infrastructure. One of the world's top seven consulting firm manages the Fund and maintains a risk-return profile that in some sense is better (less riskier) than that achieved for endowment funds set up by leading US universities like Harvard, Yale and Stanford. The Board of Trustees, chaired by the Minister of Petroleum, has the Dean of Imperial College, President of Boston University and two senior ministers as its members. A former board member has just been appointed the Energy Secretary in the US administration. A 40 strong International Advisory Committee oversees and advises on the research agenda. In the first two years of its operations, the think tank's annual budget is already more than $30 million or more tha ₹200 crore. This is the level of ambition backed up by required financial and institutional support necessary to build globally comparable policy supporting research capacity. How many think tanks or research institutes do we have in India with that kind of annual budget?

Having spent 12 years of my working life in Indian think tanks, I find the situation in the think tank world hugely disappointing and worrisome. The Indian scene is dominated by large number of tiny sized think tanks, most of whom have become personal fiefdoms of egoistic individuals and all of whom, bar a very few exceptions have been unable to build research teams who work synergistically on self-determined research agendas. India will surely suffer in its global endeavours and aspirations for this relative neglect of the knowledge sector. The trouble is that nobody in our country's establishment is thinking on these lines. While preparing the medium term strategy for Indian Council for Research on International Economic Relations (ICRIER) (of which I was the Chief Executive and Director), I met a large number of academics, industrialists and policy leaders. Only one, just one, Adil Zanulbhai, chided me for not thinking big enough and goaded me to go for a ₹500 crore ($100 million) endowment fund if ICRIER was to make a difference. I got utter disbelief and a look that implied that I had lost my bearings from some of the board members and potential donors to whom I mentioned this level of ambition. I realised that the real issue was that Indian elite is enslaved by its small mindedness and short-term goals. It refuses to think big perhaps because it does not really believe that India could be a leading knowledge producer in the world or a frontrunner in any field for that matter. Which is why we continue to look to other countries for ideas and initiatives and thrive in skilful imitation. The elite, whether in business or government, only takes a very segmented, parochial view of itself and its future and its actions are dominated by ultra short term goals.

We can for ignore the government with its perennial fiscal deficit resulting from competitive populism. But surely our corporate leaders, with their global exposure and stated desire to make India a global knowledge centre should be supporting the effort to build world class research and think tank capacities. Not at the same scale as the US or Saudi Arabia, with their vast surpluses, but at least good enough to compete with other emerging economies. It is not that the private sector does not have the financial resources to support our indigenous think thanks. They would rather support foreign think tanks and universities with established global brands. Ratan Tata, Mukesh and Anil Ambani, Anand Mahindra, N.R. Narayanmurthi, Rajan and Sunil

Mittal, Hari Bhartiya, to name only a few leading ones have donated tens of millions of dollars to US universities and think tanks all in the last 15 years. More recently, there is news of a large number of leading businessmen donating to support Brookings and Carnegie to establish their India operations. Some of these business leaders, like the Tatas, have also contributed to Indian think tanks. To this we have to add the donations by some of the IIT alumna who have donated a few million dollars to their alma maters in the last decade. But these contributions are quite dwarfed by the Indian businesses' contribution to foreign universities and think tanks. And it is not a matter of lack of absorptive capacity in the Indian institutions. Somehow, the question does not seem to cross the mind of Indian business leaders that it would perhaps serve India's cause better if they also supported indigenous think tanks, universities and research organisations as much as they were supporting the established brands and big names. Their counterparts in other emerging economies I know are doing so. The necessary trust and working relationship between the business houses and independent researchers to address India's peculiar problems and specific challenges will be built only when Indian business become more strategic in their thinking about building India's knowledge capabilities

Today, there is an acute shortage of high quality researchers and teachers in India. At the same time a very large number continue to work in foreign universities and research organisations, unable to contribute to India's challenges even when desirous of doing so. They will like to return but not at levels of remuneration and material conditions that domestic think tanks can afford to pay them given their measly financial resources and tiny endowments. Some Indian think tanks like the Centre for Policy Research are now well recognised for their globally comparable faculty and high quality output and are at the cusp of entering the global league. If they receive the additional scale up, their operations will attract a larger number of Indian scholars currently working abroad and engage foreign scholars on India specific issues. But apparently, Indian business leaders are happier building new universities and think tanks that will carry the family's name and be quite unambiguously under the day to day control of corporate house establishing them. This needs to be changed. Independently managed and autonomous research institutes carry far more credibility and provide a far more conducive environment for producing high quality output. Hopefully, Indian business leaders will soon see the merit in supporting existing institutions with revealed potential rather than or along with building their own universities or supporting foreign think tanks. Building good Indian brands in the knowledge sector is perhaps even more important for India to emerge as a leader on the global scene.

27

The Growing Trust Deficit

TO RECALL, industry leaders, nearly without exception, gave a positive public reaction to Shri Rahul Gandhi's speech at the CII's annual convention. These ranged from exceptional, brilliant, visionary containing many good elements etc. On the other hand many of us, academics, journalists, professionals found the speech to be rather unsatisfactory and a huge missed opportunity. It was in parts too general, lacked specifics, was void of even an attempt to offer solutions, did not try and lift the negative mood into which the country has undoubtedly now slipped into; was delivered in a rather cavalier manner with 'boss' being used more than a dozen times. Two questions therefore arise. One why would there be such a difference in the perception of industry leaders and the rest of us. Two, why would Mr Gandhi, who had the benefit of as much as he wanted of serious and wise counsel from the senior most echelons of the government, choose to speak as an outsider or a citizen complaining about the lack of performance and not as a leader who wants to and has ideas to set things right?

Since then, I have asked several business leaders about their reasons for their strong public appreciation of Shri Gandhi's speech. The answers have been of three types. One, a very small minority, actually liked the speech because of its frank admission of the problems, challenges and deficits facing the country. Such an admission, amounting almost to a *mea culpa* (but not quite because 'the fault was in the system' to which Shri Gandhi chose to be seen as an outsider), raised hopes that he will focus on addressing the problems, which if true would of course be most desirable. The second category of business leaders took the line they had taken with the last budget that it was good because it did not do any harm. The speech, the first ever to the industry chamber, was seen as a big step forward for a person who had virtually shunned the business class and had declared from the heights of Nayamgiri that he was only and only the voice of the excluded. And that the speech did not contain any overt or implicit threats or anti-business sentiments to establish his pro-people and left of centre credentials was a positive and good sign.

The third category of responses came from business leaders (by far the majority) who countered my question with their own of 'what else did you expect us to say about it in public?' On further prodding, they admitted to being 'afraid' of the consequences of publicly criticising any senior political leader of the ruling party let alone a probable future Prime Minister or the more powerful centre of power in case the UPA earns a third term. This response is discomforting and distressing on several counts. One, reaffirms that Delhi Durbar remains a world of smokes and mirrors where no one is prepared to be honest and straight forward and full of moral hazard. For example, an honest most competent UPA minister argued quite vehemently on one of the channels, that given the positive response of business leaders, he saw no reason for any change in policies! Isn't this dangerous and full of risks. Two, the stance by business leaders reveals their lack of appreciation of their own contribution to the country now and over the past decades. They still remain beholden to and perhaps because of the skeletons in their cupboards, truly scared of the 'long arms of the government.' The industry must recover its esteem and status in society—as it had done during the nineties and early 'noughties'. This has substantially been eroded over the last seven years, because of the torrent of malignant news of scams, unsavoury deals and the spread of crony capitalism. Three, this rather subservient posture of Indian businessmen has negative portends for any future open, transparent and constructive collaboration between the government and industry. This partnership is necessary for India to compete effectively with rising imports in the domestic market and for raising the share of Indian exports in global markets. This was beginning to happen in the latter nineties but the tide has turned and once again the industry and government find themselves not as partners but almost as adversaries, distrustful and disregardful of each other.

Having faced decades if not centuries of such adversarial government stance, the Indian industry is fully adept at and indeed a master of defensive postures. Its rather hypocritical praise of the vice president's speech demonstrates that it is now in that self preservative mode, which it adopts to wait for a better day when to spread its wings again.

Let's hope that this is untrue because it implies a reversal of the public-private partnership, which for example is the basis for Planning Commission's ambitious targets for infrastructure development. The sharp decline in fresh private investment in infrastructure projects is a pointer to this unhealthy turn of events. The onus is on the government to re-establish this trust and partnership to revert back to the higher economic growth trajectory. It will neither suffice to tell the industry that it should not be overtaken by a false sense of negativism, as the prime minister did nor does it help to raise investors' confidence to merely enumerate our past failures or recount current weaknesses that was the focus of Shri Gandhi's address. What is needed is for the government to take concrete steps to remove the fear from the minds of honest investors and businessmen so that he/she can give an honest feedback. Public-private partnership has to be a two-way affair that can prosper only in an open and transparent environment and not one in which deals are made behind closed doors. These will only invite people's righteous suspicion and indignation and erode the credibility and legitimacy of both the government and the industry—a bad omen for our future.

28

Lessons to Learn from the Uttarakhand Tragedy

DESPITE ITS HORRENDOUS scale in human suffering, the Uttarakhand tragedy is inevitably slipping down the news rankings. The media has newer pickings and the public, weighed down by its own daily chores, can hardly be expected to stick with prolonged images of grief and suffering. So it is important that at least some lessons be drawn, some minimal norms for governance be agreed upon before this earth shattering calamity is completely forgotten. It will surely not be long before the landowner-builder-contractor-politician mafia gets back to work in converting this calamity into another opportunity for raking in yet another round of ill-gotten and dishonest wealth for another round of human misery to follow. Can we not at the very least ensure by forging a minimal consensus on some norms that a repeat will not be allowed at any cost?

The very first lesson perhaps is to come out of denial and stop making a mockery of the human tragedy by coming up with absurdly low estimates of fatalities as being in hundreds or less than a thousand when even the speaker of the Uttarakhand Assembly has publicly stated them to be more than 10,000. It will do the State Administration a whole lot of credit to come up with a credible estimate that can be verified by outside agencies. At least then we would know the scale of the tragedy and the rebuilding effort that is required and mobilise the necessary resources for it. More important, as the Chinese did with their tragic earthquake in Sichuan or the Japanese with Fukishima, the real numbers if given out with the tragic respect they deserve could help weld the national conscience and build the necessary resolve to prevent another similar disaster.

This has been a national calamity and we should mark June 16 as a national disaster prevention day to annually remind ourselves to pay greater attention to disaster management and build the necessary capacities. That will allow us to take the necessary steps to populate these agencies with the relevant expertise and not just make them into sinecures for retired and defunct politicians or bureaucrats.

The second lesson is that it is completely fruitless and pointless to continue with these sterile and dysfunctional debates on development *versus* environment. There are enough examples from all over the world to show that there is no necessary trade-off between the two. In fact, if undertaken with the required degree of probity and sensitivity, development can provide the necessary resources for environment protection. There are enough examples even in our country in Madhya Pradesh, Gujarat, Himachal Pradesh and Meghalaya that demonstrate beyond doubt that development can be pursued and environment be protected simultaneously. The extremists on both sides persist with their shrill arguments and uncompromising rhetoric only to protect their petty vested interests and have no care for the public welfare or the national interest. It is time that the responsible persons from both sides of the spectrum be brought together and asked to develop a reconstruction plan for the Ganges Valley that will ensure rising living standards for the locals, provide sufficient capacities for the inevitably rising numbers of pilgrims and adventure tourists and yet protect the environment.

But the third, perhaps the most important lesson, from this horrific tragedy is that guidelines, regulations, institutions once established need to be adhered to and not be observed in their breach as is the current practice in our country. I am sure (though must admit that I have not researched into them) that there are a plethora of building guidelines, regulations and licences already in place in the Garwhal region and in each of its districts. But as we all know, the entire panoply of regulations is used to extract rents and serve as entry barriers to keep the honest developer out of the game and allow only the unscrupulous to flourish. This has resulted in the mushrooming of poorly designed tourist facilities in all the wrong places that contributed so much to this largely man-made disaster.

If we have any respect for all the thousands of lives that have been unnecessarily lost in this calamity and if we have any national self-respect, we must ensure that the reconstruction of the Valley is done in a transparent, norm based and well regulated manner. Ensuring a well regulated and transparent re-development of the Valley, is essential to restore the credibility of the government and of the political class more generally. This will not be possible by following the existing routine and leaving the task to the broken governance structure. Therefore, Chief Minister, Mr Bahuguna will do well to appoint a non-partisan Independent Monitoring Group (IMG) to come up with well considered guidelines for the reconstruction of the Valley and oversee and carefully monitor the designing and execution of the reconstruction activity in the Valley. IMG could comprise local representatives who will bring the traditional knowledge to the design table, retired media and judicial persons of known unimpeachable integrity and domain experts in development and environment.

Alternately, such monitoring and oversight can be done under the aegis of the World Bank and/or the Asian Development Bank who have already been approached for financial assistance but should also be asked to help with the oversight of the reconstruction work. The two multilateral development banks (MDBs) are committed to pursue highest ethical norms in their operations and will insist on the same if permitted to take charge of the reconstruction. This could be simpler and less politically complicated than setting up the IMG—it only requires that we stop being squeamish about temporarily handing over our local sovereignty to repair a broken governance system and set a new norm for infrastructure development.

The setting up of the IMG or handing over the task to the MDBs would ensure that the reconstruction of the Ganges Valley could become the model for all future infrastructure development in ecologically sensitive regions of the country. This will allow states like Uttarakhand, Himachal Pradesh, Arunanchal Pradesh and Jammu and Kashmir to follow the Costa Rican model of green tourism that ensure rising living standards while protecting the environment. It could be a major breakthrough in the development paradigm for these provinces. By following this suggested route, we could surely convert this tragedy into an opportunity for forging a new model of honest, clean and environmentally balanced infrastructure development in our hills. This is the only feasible way forward. It will also be a fitting tribute to all those who did not make it back home.

II

Sectoral Issues

29

Indian Industry

The Next Frontier

I WRITE THIS COLUMN from the Scottish village of Aberdour near Edinburgh, located on the Forth estuary, an idyllic location, where I am attending the plenary session of the International Futures Forum (IFF), headquartered here. IFF brings together leading specialists and experts from the widest range of disciplines that forces all participants to think laterally and be open to learning, however high the position they might well be holding in their vocation. Before trying to offer solutions, 'IFFers' undertake a learning journey, live with the problem and iterate towards a solution, working jointly with the entire range of stakeholders. Given the Indian complexity and the unique character of our ongoing multiple transition, this approach to not impose an existing model or solution but start with learning and working collectively is highly attractive.

Indian business today is in a unique situation that may not be amenable to being solved with the use of standard strategic management models. Let me elaborate. First, Indian business, in order to succeed, has to necessarily cater to the bottom of the pyramid where the purchasing power is still low but individual aspirations are high and consumers increasingly demand globally comparable products. Second, domestic business is increasingly exposed to global competition and yet has to absorb the higher cost of infrastructure and other public goods and services, including security, normally provided in other countries at relatively subsidised rates. Third, Indian industry is likely to continue to operate with serious constraints such as rigid labour markets, relatively higher costs of capital, higher transactions costs and a degree of uncertainty, as distinct from risks, in the investment environment because of the nature of domestic politics and the relatively autonomous Indian state. Fourth, there continues to be a trust deficit in the interaction between industry and public authorities that precludes a constructive interaction that would possibly result in a converged national strategy for taking India forward globally and achieving clearly defined national interests. Fifth, Indian business remains highly fragmented and an easy target for one segment being played off against the other. This prevents the industry from demanding accountability from public authorities at various levels and being constantly on the defensive even when it is universally recognised for generating value and much needed employment, striving to attain globally frontline technologies and expanding its global footprint. All these factors, which is not an exhaustive list, taken together, clearly reflect the rather unique circumstances in which Indian industry, whether in the private or public sector, finds itself today. The way forward must of course emerge from rejecting any second hand 'hand me down solutions' and having the courage to break new ground. Scotland did this when it engendered the first enlightenment with the deliberations of Smith, Hume and others in the Oyster Club. May be we in the Indian industry can help engender the second enlightenment in an attempt to find solutions for our audacious undertaking of simultaneously attempting the social, political and economic transition, a unique historical human endeavour.

In this context, the Indian corporate sector will do well to engage globally front line thinkers from a range of disciplines to help it chart out a direction for itself in an increasingly globally integrated world and identifying some tangible steps. This is hopefully already being done by large individual corporate houses but there is surely some merit in such an exercise being undertaken for the corporate sector as a whole, the results made available for a public discussion and then assisting the implementation of the lessons learnt. It may be useful to conduct such an exercise in parallel with the preparation of the country's Twelfth Five Year Plan so that India Inc could make a constructive and well considered input in to the plan process especially at a time that our planners are more open to receiving such inputs. This is a welcome development that recognises that planning in isolation of the private sector or the civil society is at best dysfunctional and at worst seriously damaging to investment environment and growth prospects. This will require that major industrial houses or premier industry chambers and associations agree to work together to support such a forward looking and analytically rich in-depth enquiry in to the future prospects and measures to address critical constraints that are currently afflicting Indian industry. Can this be possible? At least I hope so. Without such coming together of the entire Indian corporate sector, the country faces the danger of the nation's future growth being harvested by others. An unacceptable prospect because it implies an inability to generate the employment needed to constructively absorb our young labour force which in turn will result in unbearable social stresses and conflicts.

The good news is that I already notice an emerging trend in Indian business to engage with global thought leaders, of which many are Indians. Federation of Indian Chambers of Commerce and Industry (FICCI), for example, has decided to invite a global thought leader to each of its executive committee meetings. It is also trying to engage actively with futurologists in an attempt to try and anticipate the change rather than be simply overtaken by it. Clearly, the transition to look beyond the government and taking its destiny in its own hands is in progress and needs to be pushed along. A rather subversive thought! But then an IFF plenary session where all dogmas are constantly challenged evokes such thinking and hopefully will find a resonance among all the stakeholders in India's future.

30

Make Space for Private Investment in Agriculture

AGRICULTURE has emerged as the key constraint to both achieving rapid growth and improve equity. It is also clear that while land, the principal productive asset is almost entirely under private ownership, the sector is characterised by extensive government intervention and a visible lack of large scale corporate investment. As a result, the sector, except perhaps in the Punjab, Haryana and the terai region of Uttar Pradesh, remains backward. This is evident across the entire range of cultivation and irrigation practices, lack of use of new technology, non-existent back-end infrastructure and logistics, abysmal research generation and diffusion, and very low levels of processing of agro-output. No wonder with 60 per cent of population, agriculture contributes a mere 17 per cent of the GDP. This understanding must be behind the government's setting up of the Sub-Group on "Enhancing Agriculture Production and Food Security" under the Prime Minister's Council on Trade and Industry.

The Sub-Group's prime focus is to make policy recommendations for attracting greater private investment in agriculture. Surely, the real issue should not be to only attract private corporate investment but to examine the constraints that impede the inflow of private investment in agriculture. Therefore, the Sub-Group would do well to focus on these few critical constraints and lay down a time bound plan of action to address them. This will be quite different from enumerating the sub-sectors within agriculture where either private corporate investment is already present or in which it can be potentially promoted. This latter approach, which often characterises official reports and documents tends to assume private investment simply waits for a signal from the government to move into a particular sector or activity. We know from long experience that in the case of private supply response this assumption is invalid.

Private sector looks principally to prospective rate of return on its investments in conditions where risks can be managed. As Figure 30.1 shows, terms of trade have been favourable to agriculture relative to the manufacturing sector almost consistently since 1995. Unless wage costs were rising even more sharply, which did not happen, favourable movement in the terms of trade for agriculture products would demonstrate relatively higher potential rates of return on investment in agriculture. On this basis, Indian agriculture should have been attracting significant investment since the mid-nineties. Unfortunately, during the same period (1994-95 to 2008-09) the share of investment in agriculture in total national investment barely increased from 7.5 per cent to 8.4 per cent and that of private investment actually declined from 11.9 per cent in 1999-2000 to 6.4 per cent in 2007-08! Clearly, there were some severe structural factors that negated the relative price advantage and constrained investment in the agriculture sector.

It is evident that in irrigation, private investment has invariably gone for expanding the area under pump irrigation using ground water resources. Unfortunately, this has not been accompanied by sufficient public investment in recharging the aquifers and maintaining the underground reservoir. This could not be expected from the private sector. With a dramatic drop in water tables and resultant hike in irrigation costs, and especially in the context of highly erratic electricity supplies which make farmers dependent on diesel, private investment in even this form of irrigation has not increased. Moreover, this has made a complete hash of the irrigation regime that has been adopted since the green revolution. Instead, a properly working private-public partnership (PPP) could have resulted in achieving a sustainable and more inclusive irrigation practice based on regulated utilisation of continually recharged and sustainable ground water resources, eminently possible given the annual rainfall.

Figure 30.1

Food versus Manufacturing Terms of Trade

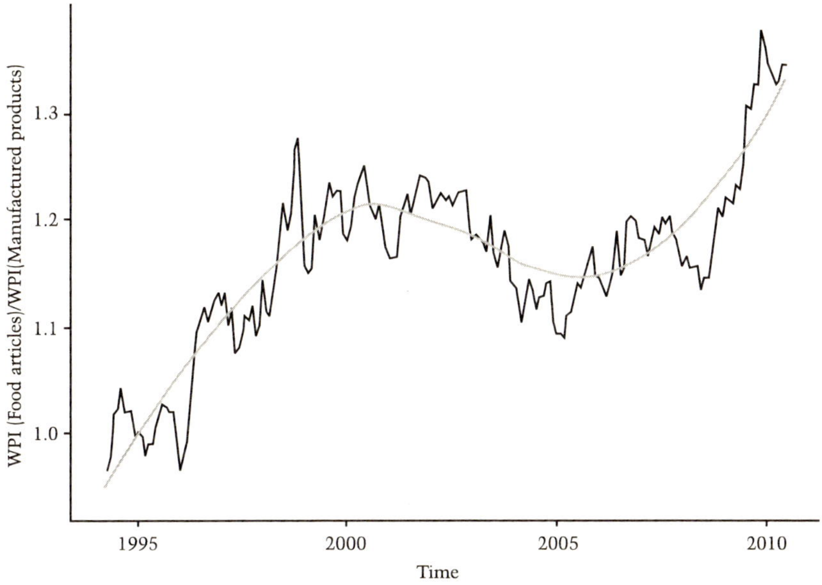

An even more important structural impediment for attracting private investment has been the pervasive presence of the government in the sector. This ranges across and is not limited to controlling foreign and domestic trade, regulating output and input prices, controlling the already distorted land market, a virtual monopoly of R&D and technology diffusion (sadly in very poor shape) and a veto on new varieties especially of genetically modified crops. This has had two very negative consequences for the entry of private investment. First, the extensive and opaque regulatory and control regime, currently in place, generates a great degree of future uncertainty for the investor. The potential investor can never be sure of the rules of the game that are constantly changing with each government decree or indecision. This pure uncertainty, very different from risk, is a death knell for investment in any sector. Agriculture can be no exception.

Second, in may sub-sectors like the *mandis,* warehousing or a number of services related to agriculture (like soil testing, pest control, veterinary services etc.), the looming presence of large public sector undertakings deters private sector entry. While due to their systemic inefficiencies these public sector agencies cannot cope with the farmers' demands and rents are collected normally, their presence combined with the administrative clout at the ground level prevents the entry of more efficient private suppliers. Unless the government is willing to bite the bullet and effectively reduce its presence in the agriculture sector, prospects of attracting greater private investment must remain rather dim. A mere statement of good intent not accompanied by action on this front will certainly not suffice.

31

Retooling India's Manufacturing Policy

MANUFACTURING is in trouble in India. The sector's share of GDP reached 16 per cent in 2006–07, then stagnated and has declined since 2010–11, to little more than 15 per cent, a sliver when compared with the shares in Thailand (36%), South Korea (31%), and China (30%). Employment in absolute terms has fallen in the formal manufacturing sector from 55 million in 2004–05 (12.2% of India's overall workforce) to 50 million in 2010 (10.5%). And the sector's growth rate has been declining for four years, actually falling into negative territory in the first quarters of 2012 and 2013.

India's development model is largely at fault. In the absence of a well-conceived policy response by the next government, manufacturing will soon be gripped by an even more profound crisis.

The sector is marked by a deep dualism—gaps between the formal and informal economies—in virtually every subsector. The dualism affects wages, productivity, technological capabilities and working conditions. This, in turn, creates capacity fragmentation, a relative absence of economies of scale and scope that renders the sector globally uncompetitive.

A disturbing feature in the past decade has been the slow but steady exit of established manufacturers, a reflection of an increasingly difficult operating environment. Many have switched to importing their products from China and elsewhere. The recently passed Land Acquisition, Rehabilitation and Resettlement (LARR) Bill, which sharply raised rural land prices and mandated a very time-consuming acquisition procedure, will likely greatly accelerate the process of de-industrialisation.

Given that India needs to find jobs for at least 1 million new workers every month for the next 15 years, the prospect of a shrinking manufacturing sector should be cause for extreme concern.

Internal Challenges

Because discussions about the problems facing manufacturing tend to begin (and end) with a long finger pointed at the government, it might be useful to start elsewhere: with constraints that flow from industry's self-induced weakness and inertia.

Indian industry continues to face an acute skills shortage. It laments this problem but does not even attempt to emulate the efforts of service sectors, which have opened large-scale in-house training programmes. It has also been unable or unwilling to adopt effective forms of collective action to demand government accountability or to find solutions for shared problems. And it has made no attempt at self-regulation to curb corrupt practices.

On another front, small and medium enterprises (SMEs) often do not receive money owed to them from their larger buyers, a far cry from the nurturing that such companies enjoy in Japan and South Korea.

Finally, because Indian industry is in large parts cartelised, there is much resistance to price competition, a short-sighted stance that hurts foreign sales.

All of these weaknesses should be addressed by the industry itself if it hopes to improve its competitiveness and credibility.

Government Policies

That said, the challenges posed, directly or indirectly, by government policies are formidable. Consider the following:

Difficult business environment. India ranked 132 out of the 185 countries in the World Bank's *Doing Business* survey in 2013. According to the official data, nearly 70 clearances are required annually for businesses to operate. The greatest cost falls on SMEs, where the proprietor has to bear the entire burden. Such an environment, combined with retroactive changes in tax demands, creates much uncertainty, anathema for investment. Another challenge is the lack of adequate protection against extortion and protection rackets.

Labor deployment rigidity. Indian manufacturing has suffered in the past from the twin constraints of militant and competitive trade unionism and a plethora of labour legislation. In recent years, unionism has ostensibly weakened. Nevertheless, it is still present in major industrial centres, and its infrequent but violent demonstration discourages foreign investors and induces others to keep employment to a minimum. India has nearly 50 laws at the central or state level that affect labour conditions. Consequently, hardly any enterprise can claim to be in total compliance.

Infrastructure deficit. The peak power deficit in India is estimated at 7 to 8 per cent, and industry is not insulated from the resultant power cuts that sweep the country. Most large manufacturing units have had to create full backup capacity, raising capital costs. Indian companies across the board bear a significantly higher price for infrastructure services and utilities than their global competitors.

Regulatory delays and lack of transparency. Over time, a rather complex regulatory structure has been established to deal with land acquisition, land use and the environment. The process has become increasingly time-consuming, opaque, and unpredictable, especially during the past 10 years under the rule of the United Progressive Alliance (UPA). According to one survey, 1,240 central and state regulations apply to the industrial sector.

Onerous commercial bank credit. More than two-third of surveyed SMEs preferred not to utilise commercial bank credit because of long processing times and stiff collateral requirements. Instead, they turned to the informal markets, paying higher rates but with less onerous conditions. This defeats the avowed aim of the government's selective credit control policy, which requires banks to earmark 10 per cent of their credit to SMEs.

What Can the Industry do?

Industry can implement a series of steps that are in its direct control.

Private companies are just beginning to tackle the skills shortages by adopting about 110 industrial training institutes. They would do well to collaborate with vocational skill providers in growing capacities, designing curricula and offering assured placements.

They should also empower their chambers and associations to take collective action to demand the timely delivery of high-quality public services. Because collective action requires credibility, they will first have to improve their record of self-regulation.

Large businesses must adopt a nurturing attitude toward their suppliers, which invariably belong to the MSME category of micro, small, and medium enterprises. And to become global players, they should substantially increase spending on research and development.

Finally, it is time to disband the thousands of sector and subsector associations whose ostensible *raison d'être* of negotiating fiscal concessions and securing government licences is increasingly irrelevant in the post-liberalisation period.

A New Government Agenda

There are two schools of opinion on the government's policy reform priorities for manufacturing. The first believes that structural conditions do not permit the growth of mass manufacturing in India. By putting a statutory floor under the price of both labour and land, the principal factors in production, the political process has effectively raised their cost. Moreover, the complicated resettlement and rehabilitation (R&R) provisions enshrined in the LARR make land procurement highly cumbersome. This school also argues that the new generation of workers, being more educated and IT savvy than earlier ones, will not accept low-productivity shop floor jobs.

Given these conditions, this school holds that India should give up trying to enter mass manufacturing and instead support 'sunrise industries'—sectors that use frontline technologies, require highly skilled labour, and are design- and technology-intensive. Government policy would focus on creating and sustaining a learning environment for businesses: India could emulate Japan and South Korea, where private firms, government science and technology agencies, and technology institutes come together to produce large-scale product and process innovations, which are then commercialised by dynamic entrepreneurs.

This is a seductive model, but a number of factors make it somewhat unfeasible, including the low R&D orientation of Indian industry and the low penetration of broadband connectivity and Internet access.

The alternative approach for policy reforms—which represents the better and more desirable way forward—is not to accept the high cost of labour and land as a given. Instead, it assumes that the large majority of new workers will continue to be semi-skilled and willing to accept productive jobs in the formal manufacturing sector (though not in the unorganised sector). Thus, this option requires government policy to be directed towards more conventional intervention.

- *Land costs.* These costs can be kept at acceptable levels by using the land already acquired by industrial development corporations in various states; increasing the ratio of floor area to space; releasing the vast stock of land owned by government and public sector entities; and amending the LARR to remove the R&R requirement for the private purchase of land.
- *Labour conditions.* It is pointless to argue for the removal of Article 35A in Chapter V of the Industrial Disputes Act (IDA) and give employers permission to hire and fire. This is a non-starter in the present Indian context. Instead, other ways have to be found for the desired level of flexibility in labour deployment. The proposal in the New Manufacturing Policy, for example, for the creation of a 'resource pool' to retrain retrenched workers and to give them unemployment security for a minimum period while they undergo the training is well worth considering. Another change would reduce the welter of labour laws to four or five comprehensive statutes.
- *Business environment.* Among the measures that could improve the environment almost immediately: introduce a combined application form for obtaining clearances, cut the time needed for starting and exiting a business, licence some private-sector banks to cater to the needs of the MSMEs.

To revive manufacturing, industry and the government (central and states) must implement a reform agenda together—to increase competition, reduce dualism, make the regulatory process more transparent and cut the compliance burden.

The two approaches described above are not necessarily in conflict. Expanding islands of innovation can coexist with a manufacturing sector that is reining in its informal side. But reforms must be urgently implemented. For if India is to achieve its strategic and development objectives, its manufacturing base can't be shrinking.

32

Management by Crisis

LET US HOPE that by the time this column appears, the Honourable Supreme Court would have lifted the complete ban on iron ore mining in Bellary district of Karnataka that it imposed on 29th July. The ban, an extreme step by any account, was imposed to demonstrate the Court's anger and disappointment at the continuing gross violation of rules and environment laws by Bellary miners and to show the Court resolve to bring these rapacious and illegal miners to heal. The Court cracked the whip despite pleas by its own Central Empowered Committee (CEC) to allow mining by public sector units and others that had been cleared by the CEC. The economic loss from a continuing ban can be enormous and aggravate the slowdown that has already gripped the economy. Nearly 21 million tonnes of steel making capacity, located in Karnataka is dependent on local iron ore supplies. Of the total production in Karnataka, which provides 24 per cent of country's iron ore output, 75 per cent comes from the Bellary-Hospet region. Shutting down Bellary mines will force a closure of the steel plants located in Karnataka as they can neither use the low grade ore from Goa nor bring in the required quantities from Jharkhand and Chhattisgarh as the high transport costs make that commercially infeasible.

The closure of Karnataka steel plants will result in huge commercial losses to these companies but the far bigger impact will be in the loss of production and employment in downstream industries such as automobiles, consumer durables, machine tools and engineering products. Direct employment loss would itself be about 80,000 with several lakh other jobs being jeopardised in downstream industries. The government stands to loose ₹10,000 crore in revenues and commercial banks could suffer an asset deterioration of up to ₹50,000 crore. It is evident that even excluding other relatively lesser losses to railways, state government and utilities, the negative economic impact of a continued ban on mining in Bellary, may be just too large for the economy to absorb at this stage when investors' sentiment is already frail and global conditions are becoming ominous. The ban, if continued, will bring the Indian economy to the edge of the avoidable precipice!

In imposing the ban, the Supreme Court is presumably acting on the basis of its past experience. The Court saved Delhi from choking to death from noxious transport exhaust fumes by insisting on a cut-off date for the introduction of CNG in public transport vehicles. This created a mini-crisis with the entire Delhi transport system grinding to a halt for a few weeks. Necessary executive action then followed. The Court therefore realises that in India, we follow the practice of 'Management by Crisis!' Far from acting in anticipation of emerging situations, how so ever clearly visible, action is postponed until the time has virtually run out—creating avoidable pressures and incurring unnecessary costs. But given the predominant culture of management by crisis, the Court, acting purely on practical logic, has again decided to create a crisis, and one which is far larger in its coverage and impact than stopping the Delhi public transport in its tracks. Executive action will hopefully follow. Can we really afford such repeated crisis which seems to be a necessary condition for generating the required policy response and action?

The impending crisis in mining, of gigantic proportions is now starkly visible and will extend to all mining including iron ore, coal, bauxite, copper and other minerals. Business as usual will result in foregoing the use of our very large reserves of these natural resources that are essential ingredients for industrialisation and growth. A very large part of these reserves lie either under forest cover or under lands populated by indigenous people. All these will be out of bounds for commercial mining, which is dominated by rapacious miners who are continually thwarted by social pressure and judicial action. Such an outcome will be disastrous. We will have to then import massive volumes of these minerals, putting unsustainable pressure on our balance of payments, rendering our industries uncompetitive and generating massive loss of employment. The Honourable Court would do well to put together a group of relevant experts and industry personnel to find a way out of this impending disaster and save the country from ruination. Two suggestions can be made here for a possible way forward. One, to immediately establish three technically competent and Independent regulators, one each for iron ore, coal and other minerals respectively. These regulators by drawing up the necessary regulations and enforcing them strictly will de-politicise the sector and minimise violations of environment laws and rights of the tribal people. Second, the government has to ensure that its policy framework attracts large, organised, technologically well-equipped and socially and environmentally conscious mining companies. These are more susceptible to public pressure and less prone to corruption and illegal ways of operating a business. There are some elements in the draft mining law, as it exists today, which could have the opposite effect of driving out the large and organised miners from the sector and encourage those who are rapacious, only want to scour the land, ride roughshod over peoples' rights and have zero concern for the environment. This would only result in India being unable to take advantage of its own natural resources. This will indeed be a case of denying ourselves the natural advantage simply because we are unable to jettison our culture of managing by crisis!

33

Beyond FDI in Multi-Brand Retail

FOREIGN DIRECT INVESTMENT (FDI) in multi-brand retail is hopefully a done deal. I sincerely hope that saner counsels will prevail on Friday and the government will be steadfast. More importantly, the opposition will not encourage traders to take to the streets and spoil the image of our country as an investment destination. Talks of reversing the law in the coming years is irresponsible. This long drawn saga has raised several questions that go far beyond the mere issue of FDI in retail.

The first question is about the political class's continued perception that an anti-foreigner stance is a populist one and yields political dividends. After more than six decades of untrammelled sovereignty; with the external sector now accounting for more than 50 per cent of our GDP as compared to a mere 16 per cent prior to the 1991 reforms; with more than 10 million Indians resident abroad; and the unambiguous and repeatedly demonstrated acceptance of foreign born persons as social icons and political leaders at the highest level; this anti-foreigner jingoism and rhetoric can no longer be attributed to our history. Yes the spectre of the East India Company continues to be is raised in many discussions on FDI, but it regularly fails to evoke any significant response. Our political leaders must recognise that the majority of Indians, born after 1980, more than three decades after our independence, do not perceive any threat to India's sovereignty and security from the proverbial 'foreign hand'. If at all they are concerned about the threat to our sovereignty from internal sources in the face of slowdown in growth and employment. Let the ghost of the East India Company be finally exorcised from our body politic.

The second question relates to our leaders' propensity to try and justify all policy action and indeed non-action in terms of its impact on the *'aam aadmi'* presumably the poor. Agriculture reforms will be undertaken and electricity will be supplied free even if the small and marginal farmer's meagre land holdings means that she/he cannot afford to have an electric irrigation pump. Inaction on fuel subsidies, non-rationalisation of railway passenger fares and continued distortion of fertiliser prices are all justified similarly. So on this occasion as well, the opposition has waxed eloquently on the demise and deprivation of the small trader, the *kirana* merchant as a result of the entry of the *firangi* retailer. Nothing could be more misleading. Can anyone claim that the proverbial intrepid Indian merchant from Munshi Prem Chand's stories, is a member of the deprived masses? Does it not challenge reason to believe that owners of mom and pop stores, by far the most politically networked and organised segment, will simply buckle under. They have held their own so far against Indian giants. Do they really need policy protection when they thrive on unregulated conditions and actively participate in parallel markets? Is it not, therefore, really hypocritical to portray them as victims? Their share, from all available estimates, will remain at 80 per cent or more of a market that promises to double in the next 20 years to grow to a size of a whopping $820 billon.

It is of course true that our *nagarshets* and *vanik rajas* that go back to the days of the Vaishali and Magadh kingdoms have taken goods to Europe across the silk road. The remnants of a Hindu Dharamshala in Baku, to which I was taken, is glorious testimony to that. The question is whether the Indian trader, who was used to supplying to the courts and *durbaris,* in India or abroad, has the know-how and capacity and indeed the will to raise scales manifolds, reduce margins per unit and meet the exponentially expanding consumption demand of the growing middle classes in India. From all existing anecdotal and survey based evidence, the answer has to be a resounding no.

The disappointment in this debate has been that the opposition is happy to fight the previous battle. The real danger to the mom and pop stores is not from the large format, suburban based, difficult to access super markets and multi-brand retailers. The real danger is emerging in the form of e-Commerce, the Flipkart, Jabong and

Amazons of the world. These retail business models cut at the very root of the competitive advantage of the *kirana* stores by delivering goods to the homes of the consumers and accepting payment on delivery. Soon enough some intrepid Indian trader will start to supply daily necessities on-line and maintain an on-line credit account. That will sound the death knell of the neighbourhood convenience store. I am convinced our *kirana wallas* are already preparing their response to this development. Yet our political leaders are gypped into believing that the large format store, which complements the *kirana* store is the problem.

Finally, the question arises if the FDI victory heralds the onset of more reforms and the change in the DNA of the UPA from a left of centre, populist party of the 'excluded' to one that promotes rapid growth, undertakes economic and social modernisation and improves public services delivery? I am afraid the test for that still remains to be the handling of the fiscal deficit situation in the country. The victory in the bruising FDI battle could give the momentum for taking much needed hard decisions on reducing subsidies that essentially benefit the middle classes. The danger is that having re-furbished its reformist credentials, the UPA could well pressurise its government to implement a plethora of populist measures to ensure electoral success. The cost of that populism will hugely dwarf the gains from allowing FDI in multi-brand retail.

34

Bring Back Privatisation Where Necessary

The Air India saga goes on endlessly. There is no possibility of airlines' continued survival except on the basis of open ended and unlimited budgetary allocations. Its accumulated losses (before tax) for the three years 2007-08 to 2009-10 are more than ₹15,000 crore. Its net worth, despite repeated capital infusion by the government was negative, ₹4,481 crore in 2009-10 and it employs 256 personnel per aircraft against the industry average of 156! The various turnaround plans prepared by outside agencies and experts are virtual non-starters as their implementation requires a modicum of normal corporate behaviour that is apparently not possible in the prevalent politically vitiated and demoralised environment. The Maharaja is not just sick, it seems to have entered a stage of terminal decline. It will be unfair for the government to now ask public sector banks, led by the State Bank of India, to mobilise funds for equity participation in the company. Unlike the Kingfisher airlines, where such an approach has been adopted, there is no viable plan or strategy in place or even in sight to bring Air India back to profitability. Not only Air India's net worth is negative, it has huge outstanding payables to other public sector entities like the oil companies and airports authority. There is danger that this one haemorrhaging company could pull others down with it as well.

Air India has been financially bankrupt for the last several years. As private company it would have been closed long ago. Its continued operation with access to virtually unlimited amounts of public resources is a source of major distortions in the industry and could effectively prevent any Indian airlines company from becoming globally competitive. Not only does the continued subsidisation of Air India precludes a rationalisation of capacities and market shares which would allow other competitors to take advantage of economies of scale and scope, it also creates substantial moral hazard problems for the industry. This has been amply visible in other airlines being unable to rationalise their workforce and getting away with less than globally acceptable levels of efficiency, safety and customer care requirements. With airline traffic growing at an amazing 20 per cent or more annually, Indian airlines have the opportunity to challenge globally established majors in the airline industry. However, this opportunity will be squandered if government policy remains exclusively focused on saving and resuscitating Air India rather than be concerned with the global competitiveness of Indian airlines industry as a whole.

The way forward is amply clear and has been suggested on numerous occasions by political leaders, industry experts and sundry observers. But this requires the utterance of the currently dreaded and politically incorrect 'P Word'. Privatisation of inefficient and haemorrhaging public sector enterprises has been banished from the Indian policy lexicon for some years. Disinvestment is the most that we can talk about and that too in undertones for fear of being seen as politically incorrect. But as Air India's case demonstrates in ample measure, one cannot substitute for the other. In Air India's case the only possible way forward is to sell the company, privatise it, to any willing buyer which may itself be difficult to locate. Privatising Air India or selling it to a strategic investor should not be politically or ideologically unacceptable. The airlines does not provide a public service to the under-privileged. It does not cater to some strategic needs except for ferrying stranded Indians, which could be achieved by chartering private flights. Air India's employees certainly do not represent the 'have-nots.' Its management has not covered itself with glory either. It serves no strategic or security objective. So why has privatisation being ruled out ab-*initio* as an option? To my mind there are none. Instead, the corporation is a prime case for privatisation and has been for decades. It is time that the public exchequer and the Indian taxpayer is rid of this completely unnecessary burden. There are clearly no short-cuts. Even the alternative of handing over the management to a private company while retaining government ownership is not feasible at this stage as employees will continue to act as government servants with minimal accountability and potential investors will remain wary of government intervention. The truth is that Air India can either be closed down or privatised to save the country not only of financial waste but also of avoidable future embarrassments.

There are only two possible reasons for not privatising the airline. One that it is our national carrier carrying the Indian flag. Private airlines can carry the same flag with the same degree of pride if not more. Are we any less proud of Tatas, L&T and Mittals having acquired international status than we are of BHEL, EIL and NTPC emerging as globally competitive players? Two, that it serves vital national interests in flying to destinations which will not be catered to by private airlines. This can surely be easily and far more economically addressed by earmarking a pool of public funds to be paid to those airlines which fly to commercially non-viable destinations. This will also eliminate major distortions that are generated in the industry when a dominant player is allowed to operate without a hard budget constraint. This is anathema to competition. The Competition Commission of India should take up this case up on a *suo moto* basis and help the government out of its present predicament.

35

Business Lobbies Must Shape up for Growth

JUST THREE YEARS AGO, India was viewed as another Asian upcoming economic giant, along with China. Now, instead, the country is in a severe economic slowdown with a potential balance of payment (BoP) crisis. The economy is in serious danger of slipping into a long period of 'slowflation' that will combine sub-5 per cent GDP growth with near double digit retail inflation. This has the potential for generating unbearable social stress as employment opportunities dry up and the demographic dividend begins to turn in to a demographic disaster

Certainly New Delhi's economic mismanagement is largely to blame. But so is the Indian business community. In the last few years, it has abdicated the role it has historically played in providing the government with an independent opinion and pushing for the critical reforms required.

There is a clear opportunity for corporate India to step up and pull the country out of the current crisis by proactively altering its approach to government inaction. Top-of-the-list is reform of the apex chambers of commerce. These have become insiders' clubs and event managers at best, rather than the representative voice of the wider business community. This is particularly important now, when our weak 4.5 per cent growth rate will probably dip further. Setting their own house in order will reinstate the legitimacy lost over the years. Only then can they credibly push governments for change.

The chambers must also ensure that they mediate the suggestions coming from their member so as to make them compatible with broader industry interests and also in line with the national interest. For example, instead of repeating ad-nauseum their demand for labour hire and fire policies, impractical in any case in the present political scenario, business would have done well to ask for better working conditions in the informal sector of the economy where working conditions can be shocking and wages below the minimum stipulated. This would give business the legitimacy to ask for greater flexibility in labour deployment.

The chambers played almost no role in the formulation of the unaffordable Food Security Act (FSA) and the Land Acquisition Act, the latter of which will surely stymie business expansion. Nor did they insist on clear infrastructure outcomes from the work assigned by the NREGS, also a funds-guzzler. Instead of putting forward a well-researched paper that showed how enterprise can help to efficiently develop industrial and agricultural infrastructure to ensure food security, the chambers merely opposed the food bill or recommended fixing the distribution system before the passing of the bill—all to no avail. They did press for subsidies to be reduced, again a consideration that New Delhi ignored. By the time the legislation was passed, it was too late. And in a direct reflection of this economic mismanagement private investment has come to a virtual standstill and share of investment in GDP has declined from 38 per cent in 2007 to 35 per cent in 2012. What's left is an entitlement-driven economy supported by taxpayer money, with policies now hard to overturn or reform. Like Brazil in 1985, this can lead to a fiscal crisis—the last thing business wants.

India's business community must take responsibility for long-term structural changes. It must endeavour at all times to ensure that Indian business becomes globally competitive and pressurise the government to implement the required policies to help them in this critical effort. It must not revert to its old 'Bombay Club' instincts when it regarded India as its protectorate, demanding preferential treatment over multinational competitors and lobbying to shut out imports. Indeed all businesses in India, including multinationals, must have a level playing field and there should be no talk of reversing the free trade agreements (FTAs) that we have already entered into.

This refreshing change will only happen if the chambers honestly restructure themselves. Their focus must stay on advising the government on business policy, looking beyond the interests of a few powerful members, independently funding their organisations, and supporting their lobbying with serious research. The most important step perhaps is to make the chambers completely independent from financial support from the government both at the Centre and the states. It can be easily seen that with an increasing share of revenues coming from government sources, the chambers tend to be diffident in raising their voices in opposition to policies that they clearly see as not being in the national interest. This virtually destroys the relevance of the chambers in putting forward viable policy options for the government's considerations.

Another necessary condition for the chambers to restore their credibility and legitimacy is to to self-regulate themselves such that their membership is not open to those who are either convicted or those who have over time developed a public reputation for unethical behaviour. With the Supreme Court's judgement for not permitting convicted politicians from holding public office or to be elected to the parliament, now in effect, it is essential for business to implement such a provision if it wishes to retain the confidence of the general public.

Finally, chambers must ensure that their membership is as broad based as can be and is representative of all the strata of Indian business. Germany provides a good model. There, all companies are required to be members of one of the 80 chambers, which in turn are part of the single Association of German Chambers of Commerce and Industry, an inclusive and politically powerful group. In India, only 7,100 companies are members of the by far the largest apex chamber, the Confederation of Indian Industry (CII), despite there being an additional at least 26 million micro, small and medium enterprises, just 5 per cent of which are officially registered. CII, FICCI (Federation of Indian chambers of Commerce and Industry) and ASSOCHAM (Associated Chambers of Commerce and Industry of India) are not reflective of the multi-layered landscape of Indian enterprise which comprises these vibrant but voiceless smaller ventures. It is also important to ensure that complete transparency is maintained in the process of granting membership and in the election of the office bearers of the chambers. This alone will ensure that these chambers are taken seriously by the government and the civil society.

A last word: the post of chamber president is reserved for those who seek it, typically business owners of large enterprises looking for access to the corridors of power. Better to follow instead the United Kingdom (UK), where the chief spokesperson is a professional, not a business owner, enabling him or her to represent the independent views of a broad set of businessmen without the baggage of vested interests.

Business activism, that reconciles business interest with the broader national interest is the need of the hour. This will take us back to the times when business worked closely with leaders of India's independence movement in complete trust and transparency. Only then will corporate India regain its lost legitimacy, and India, its lost growth and global competitiveness.

III

Reforms and the Political Process

36

Identity Politics

A Shameful, Dangerous Game

IT IS THAT TIME again when all of us Indians should hang their heads in shame. What has happened in Muzzaffarnagar is beyond mere repentance and regret. It is a national shame and we should have our national flag at half mast all over Uttar Pradesh (UP) and indeed in Delhi for the next month in the memory of the victims and also to ensure that governments in Lucknow and Delhi, do not easily forget their culpability in this totally avoidable tragedy. Our political parties should resolve to not send their glib spokespersons (offensive on times in their arrogance and compulsion to shift blame) to any TV discussion on this issue as that just helps to trivialise this horrific act. Instead, they should be introspecting and examining their role in this latest episode of sub-human behaviour. We should impress upon our government and political leaders that government energies should rather be spent on putting an end to this cycle of communal violence and identity politics rather than vying for a seat in the UN Security Council (UNSC). Will it behove India to be a member of the UNSC, while thousands are internally displaced and human rights are routinely violated in hundreds of incidents of communal violence every year?

Having experienced it first hand in 1984, I can imagine the extent of human despair and cold fear when one feels completely vulnerable realising that there is no protection from the marauding gangs and one simply waits to be killed or worst still be burnt alive or be converted overnight into life-long refugees. All those horrific images that I had thought I have banished from my consciousness come rushing back—of children traumatised, of women unable to save their dignity and men having to change their appearances to avoid certain death. How can our politicians, who act with such cold calculus to let matters take their own course, not realise that their behaviour amounts to treason against the Indian Republic because each time such bloodletting happens it palpably weakens the already fragile social fabric of this country. With each communal riot, divisions deepen in the psyche and hearts of our people and surely if this deepening continues, physical separation cannot be prevented. Yet our politicians do not hesitate to add fuel to fire and bake their electoral bread in the fires that devastate homes and ruin lives forever. My real fear is that the expectation that such incidents will become rarer over successive generations and with improvement in living standards appears to be misplaced. If anything, greater material prosperity seems to be providing more resources to fuel the frenzy and more dangerous weapons to exact the highest toll of human lives. Clearly, we need conscious, deliberate collective action to remove this malignancy from our society. Who will lead the effort is the question before it is once again too late.

There is always the blame game and shouting matches, on television channels on who started it all. But does that really matter? What is it that makes the other side react in such a ferocious and sub-human manner? And why does not the administration whose bounden duty it is to prevent such carnage and if possible nip it in the bud act in time? The failure of the State to do its job and accept responsibility is nauseous. This is a State, which has been debilitated by the venal ambitions of those who hold its offices and who will not flinch from leading it to complete paralysis and inaction if that served their immediate purpose.

Two questions arise. First, to what extent is the identity politics of our political parties either in the name of secularism or on openly opportunistic grounds responsible for the continued communal violence in our country. Second, is there any practical way in which the state machinery can be insulated from the consequences of identity politics. I am sure there are many complex determinants of identity politics. The growing social malaise caused by poor quality of education, declining moral norms and rampant corruption amongst political leaders and their bureaucratic henchmen surely contribute to perpetuating this vicious form of identity politics.

However, I think that the principal factor for continued expansion of identity politics comes from the rent seeking nature of a growing number of political workers at all levels. I hear about cases of liquor being sent to community leaders for municipal council and university union elections, let alone legislative and parliamentary elections. Surely that is done in the expectation of mobilising particular communities by whatever means and then earn a hefty return once in office. For a large majority who have joined politics (and unfortunately for an increasing number in senior bureaucracy as well), the sole objective is to secure the people's mandate to get into office and then use it without any compunction to maximise private gains and raid the exchequer. These political functionaries (they cannot and should not called leaders), who are opportunists to the core, have no concern whatsoever for people's welfare or for the progress of our country or indeed the challenges it may be facing. This must change.

The change could begin if we squarely face the question of a possible trade-off between the politics of so-called secularism (which in effect become a euphemism for identity politics) and politics of good governance and development. As far as I can see, political parties have used the excuse of safeguarding secularism to almost wilfully neglect economic development. This serves their purpose rather well because economic backwardness traps the youth in the clutches of identity-based politicians who then use them as cannon fodder. We are witnessing a frightening trend towards the lumpenisation of our youth, from Srinagar to Muzzaffarnagar. This is a direct consequence of slow pace of development, poor skilling and scarcity of jobs. It is time that the electorate gives a resounding rebuff to those who practice identity politics. We should force our politicians to focus only and only on development, good governance and employment generation. It is time that we start the process of putting into the dustbin of history all those who want to make their fortunes by dividing our people, robbing them of their human dignity and endangering this country's destiny.

37

Governance Rot

I AM WRITING this column from Malgund, located on the Konkan coast near Ganapatipule, 25 kms from Ratnagiri, the proposed site of the Areva nuclear power plant. We have been coming here since 1989, initially every year, for our week long Sahaja Yoga meditation convention over Christmas. This time, because of the telecom revolution the internet and the spread of 'dish antennas', the outside world has come crashing in on us, taking away the relative isolation that we had always looked forward to in the past. However, the remote location, surrounded by mango orchards and waves that are incandescent at night because of the phosphorus coastal rocks, along with the tenuous connectivity with the rest of the country has provided the right setting for year-end reflection.

The sharpest memory of the year gone by is that of the dangerously increasing governance deficit; of government losing the plot and of its legitimacy being constantly challenged and eroded. This is reflected across many dimensions. There is the huge infrastructure deficit exemplified by long hours of power cuts; the state of our national highways and even more so the secondary roads. The lack of any discipline or basic civic sense with no visible attempt by public authorities to rectify this; the collapse of law and order and threat to personal security that has been so vividly brought out by the shocking gang rape of the 23 year old; the fact that provision of private security services is now one of the fastest growing industries in the country. The utter impunity with which our political leaders, businessmen and leading members of the national elite continue to flout the prevailing laws of the country whether it is in grabbing land on false pretexts, laundering money to tax havens and in general abusing their power to the extent possible. The Ponty Chaddha murder and the series of rapes in the heart of the nation's capital exemplify the collapse in governance across large parts of the country. In Malgund, this rather sleepy village with its *Apus* mango groves, the collapse can be seen in the huge traffic chaos that prevails around the Ganesha temple in nearby Ganapatipule, which is constantly on the brink of violence as the rising tide of religious tourists descend on the place and left largely to their own ingenuity with public authorities conspicuous by their absence. There is a widening chasm between private sector growth and delivery of public services and infrastructure which will result in a major disaster with unpredictable consequences.

The government and political leadership is expected to be the vanguard of the society and anticipate emerging trends and respond appropriately. In India today, the government and especially our political leadership not only fails to anticipate the emerging needs and aspirations of the people but waits until a crisis to respond. This is the worst kind of 'political tailism.' This is a result of the establishment's refusal to give up populism that impels it to dodge every problem until it erupts as a crisis. The danger is that with rising aspirations and growing impatience this strategy of 'management by crisis' is becoming not only increasingly unviable but indeed dangerous.

Can this spreading governance rot not be prevented? Are we destined to go down the path of complete government illegitimacy and governance breakdown that will result in the 'survival of the fittest'? Let us hope not. The price we will have to pay for such an eventuality would be unacceptably high. There is a glimmer of hope and coincidentally, as happened in the run-up to the emergency in 1973-74, it comes from Gujarat. The 'nav nirman yuvak samiti aandolan' caught the peoples' imagination, and gave them the courage to stand up against the prevailing corruption and misrule in the state. It finally brought Jai Prakash Narain out in opposition to the ruling dispensation of the time. This time it is Narendra Modi's third victory that provides us the ray of hope in as much as it demonstrates quite unequivocally that good economic policies combined with disciplined and honest administration can also yield good electoral outcomes. This experience could well be repeated in Madhya Pradesh and Chhattisgarh in the 2013 elections. All three happen to be Bharatiya Janta Party (BJP) ruled states. The party will do itself, and indeed the country, a huge disservice if it failed to build on this success in the three states and project their model as a nationwide alternative. This would be in sharp contrast to the UPA's model, which relies almost exclusively on rank populism, irrespective of its economic consequences as its principal electoral strategy.

The chief ministers of these states, Narendra Modi, Shivpal Singh Chauhan, Raman Singh and the likely incoming chief minister of Rajasthan, Ms Vasundra Raje should come together to offer an alternative paradigm for the country. This would emphasise forward-looking and growth-oriented policies and a solid programme of good governance, which will effectively address the trade-off between growth and equity. Given that the electoral result in Gujarat has preceded the other three, Narendra Modi could take the lead in articulating the alternative paradigm. With this one move, Mr Modi would shed his provincial image and emerge as a pan-India leader. He will also convey the message to political pundits and media gurus that it is a mistake to use history for predicting the future in India, where history is being constantly overtaken by current developments.

38

Fighting the Corruption Demon

WITH THE EXPOSURE by the Italian authorities of the bribery payments in the Augusta-Westland helicopter deal, another scam comes to light. However, the negative news neither stops for nor does it deter the heads of governments who continue to make a beeline for Delhi with their gaze fixed on lucrative potential deals and opportunities in the growing Indian market with its rising middle class and the largest volume of defence imports. In a way, this reflects the cynicism of our foreign friends for whom it seems 'everything goes' as long as a deal can be clinched. These presidential and prime ministerial visits no longer capture the public attention, which is riveted on the continued saga of corruption, bribery, misappropriation and rent seeking at an unprecedented scale. I have no doubt that this has continued for ever in our country. It is indeed ironical that so much has come to light during the regime of a prime minister who is personally honest to a fault. My bewilderment is on account of his silence and lack of precipitate action against those who he must know are perpetrators of these criminal acts. The only explanation I have for Dr Manmohan Singh's inaction against such rampant corruption and despite the huge outcry against it that he is in one way or the other effectively barred from taking action against his cabinet colleagues, coalition partners or against senior members of this own party. This is indeed a pity because it will be the supreme irony that a man like him could well be remembered by posterity for having overseen perhaps the most corrupt period in the country's post independence history. I urge him to take the needed steps to prevent such a denouement.

An argument, often made, is that rent seeking and even large scale corruption is a part and parcel of the market economy with minimal adverse consequences. For example, corruption, we are told, is widespread in China but it has an enviable growth record. I don't agree. Such a cynical attitude is in my view adopted by us because we would like to continue with the status quo rather than be bothered about the corruption and think of doing something about it. We in the middle class want to get on with our life and to be able to do so, we simply choose to ignore corruption and its unholy aftermath in the form of continuous erosion of moral values in the society. Some like Kejriwal take up the issue but are quickly seen to be using this for furthering their own political ambitions. The credibility is soon lost and people revert back to their cynical ways.

Some friends argued that the combination of a strident anti-corruption electronic media and the public movement launched by Anna Hazare and Kejriwal's India Against Corruption, pointed to the arrival of India's progressive moment. Comparisons to a similar period in the US history at the turn of the 20th century were quickly drawn. However, it soon became clear, that in our case, a very substantial segment of media owners were themselves even more cynical and quite at peace with rampant corruption. Some in fact are apparently thriving in it! I was recently horrified to hear of a large media house virtually blackmailing very established industrialists to advertise on its channels and print outlets while encouraging its self-righteous television anchor to launch tirades against corruption. This is extreme hypocrisy. I am told by journalists friends that the practice of paid news and arm twisting of businessmen and political leaders by media tycoons for commercial gain is widespread across electronic and print media and in both English and vernacular languages. It saddens me to know that the common Indian citizen, who sets so much store by the media's role in our society is destined to be disillusioned. Indians, it seems can simply find no succour from the large scale, widespread and deeply entrenched corruption across all sections of our society. Unfortunately, there is no Indian progressive moment in sight, at least not from where I can see it.

But such a situation also frightens me. Setting aside the moral dimension for a moment, important though it is, we can see that such high level of corruption may be acceptable only until living standards of the majority are improving on the back of rapid economic growth. When growth begins to falter as it is doing at present and living standards fall and unemployment rears up its ugly head again, the frustration of the people can boil over. This can take several unpredictable forms—further strengthening of left wing extremism; rising tide of religious fundamentalism and terrorism; increasingly violent sons of soil movements; widespread lumpenisation combined with vigilantism that challenges the law and order system. Any such outcome, will push the country back several years if not decades and could even take us into completely unchartered and dangerous territories.

On the other hand, by stamping out rampant corruption and achieving rapid and inclusive growth, India could well be an exemplar for other emerging and developing economies. I hope that is not too much to expect. I am sure Dr Manmohan Singh recognises the very high stakes involved and will, even at this stage of prime ministership, launch a serious drive against corruption especially that of the political class. He will have the entire people's support against any coterie, howsoever powerful it might be, that tries to thwart him in this effort. The principal opposition party must also make anti-corruption the central plank of their election manifesto. This used to be the BJP's USP in an earlier era. But now they will have to try very hard to convince the electorate that this is not yet another cynical attempt to hoodwink them. Given the widespread disillusionment and cynicism, it will not be easy. But surely it can be and must be done.

39

Let the Parliament Work!

THE FIRST DAY of the winter session of the Parliament was again lost without any business being transacted. There are ominous signs that political opportunism from all sides will again result in a logjam that will further debilitate the executive and bring no succour to those wanting tangible action to revive the economy. We may be truly hurtling towards a precipice from which it will be very difficult and costly to lift the economy and put it back on track.

It is not just economic management which is in poor shape. Recent events have demonstrated that there is now an extensive failure of our political and administrative apparatus that faces the dangers of losing its legitimacy and be seen as serving the interests of a small nexus that has effective control over state resources and openly flout the law and coerce the State functionaries into taking illegal and morally reprehensible actions. As a result of this State capture by the lumpens and crony capitalists, we the ordinary citizens increasingly feel disempowered and disenfranchised. Given the impunity with which the State functionaries act to quell the rights of its citizens, whom they are meant to serve, shows that we still have the vestiges of the colonial state, which we inherited and have been unable to replace with a modern, democratic and accountable entity.

The panoply of dysfunctional laws and rules that the State has armed itself with effectively ensures that each one of us, perhaps with the exception of a handful of ruling families and groups, live in mortal fear of being declared a 'criminal' and be 'picked up' or 'raided' at the mere whim and fancy of a highly placed official or political big-wig. Is this the democracy that the leaders of our national movement fought and died for? It is critical that this be accomplished soonest before the *aam aadmi*, increasingly frustrated by the ongoing non-governance and high handedness of petty officials opts for less democratic options, in the hope that like in the East Asian countries, these will at the least afford it a much faster rise in their living standards.

The patently illegal arrest of two young women in Mumbai for the mere act of expressing their honest and harmless opinion reveals the continued non-accountability of our State apparatus and smacks of a colonial 'ruler and ruled' mindset among our police and civil servants. The two were charged with a non-bailable offense of spreading religious hatred, when they were simply saying that they did want Mumbai to be shut down for any one person. Is it not the ultimate irony that attacks on their homes and the pressure on the police to arrest the two young women was carried out by those who have made their political career by spreading communal hatred against one-seventh of our population and have physically assaulted their fellow citizens in an effort to drive them out of Mumbai only because their parents were born in another part of India! And to top it all, while the media took up gross injustice, there is not a word of contrition or censure from the high priests of Indian political establishment. The sentiment we were told is 'what is new?'

The macabre shoot out at Chattarpur farms on the outskirts of Delhi that resulted in the violent deaths of two brothers again showed up the complicity of the State apparatus in illegal activity. The two brothers, have become 'famous' for having built their vast and unestimable business empire in record time by using all the means that exemplify the worst aspects of crony capitalism and which benefit from the unholy nexus between unscrupulous politicians and unethical businessmen. And yet these brothers were provided their personal security by the police force of at least two states *viz.*, Uttar Pradesh and Punjab. These policemen who were deputed to 'protect' these brothers were present at the farm at the time of the shootout. In addition the two brothers' private security guards were armed to their teeth in brazen violation of all stated laws and norms. How can this happen without the active connivance and perhaps collusion of several branches of the State apparatus? Does it not show that the State has been effectively captured by those who do not conform to the stated law of the land?

I recently asked a business friend of mine, living in NOIDA, about why he was not seizing the clearly visible opportunities for growth. His answer shocked me as he said that he was not interested because of the fear that this will attract the attention of the Ghaziabad mafia with all its unsavoury consequences for not just him but the family. He would rather expand his operations abroad where his personal security was more assured. Can we really hope to raise our growth rates, generate the necessary employment and eliminate poverty when our ordinary businessmen live in daily fear of their personal and family security? Can we have any progress when honest civil servants trying to implement the law of the land are transferred every six months and worse still professionals get simply murdered by the mafia when he tries to stop the use of kerosene for diesel adulteration.

Today we are experiencing not only the inability of the government to provide an equitable access to public education and health that is a feature of any modern democracy. We are seeing a capture of the State by the lumpen and crooked rich. This can result rather quickly into a complete de-legitimisation of the entire State structure and surely that of the executive and legislatures, with unpredictable adverse consequences. India cannot be allowed to descend into a state of extensive governance failure and a de-legitimisation of the State itself. The political class must realise that the costs of picking up the pieces could be enormous and perhaps unbearable. The time to act is now. For starters, the Parliament should be allowed to function to avoid further erosion of State's legitimacy.

40

Empowering the *Aam Aadmi*

THE *AAM AADMI* season is again with us. It will continue until the budget session is over and during which the entire political class will either claim to have acted in the interest of this elusive entity—the common man or be criticised for not doing so. A majority of policies and vast volumes of public expenditure is supposedly spent on improving the lot of the *aam aadmi*. Yet I have never seen anywhere even an attempt at defining this central object of all policy making and political action and public handouts. Perhaps it is better to leave him/her undefined because it is clear that just like perfect competition the *aam aadmi* is only a concept, not to be ever found in reality. It is used as a kind of benchmark for gauging the popular acceptability of policies being proposed. This is a dangerous practice because it encourages populism at the cost of policies which are based on sound economics that can unambiguously improve the welfare of the majority especially the poor. Some examples will help.

The under recoveries from sale of kerosene during April to September 2012 are a huge ₹14,331 crore (MOP Report, Jan 2013). This subsidy, which is perhaps a bit lower, is supposed to help the *aam aadmi*. It is officially accepted that more than a third of the kerosene sold is used for adulterating diesel and petrol. Large proportion of kerosene is diverted for commercial use and only a small amount used by actual consumer. The really poor and needy is condemned to use either firewood, cow dung pats or simply waste material, which they collect by foraging far and wide. An alternative use of the kerosene subsidy could be spend the entire amount for scholarships to the children from BPL (below poverty line) families. This can be better monitored, have lower leakages and create capabilities that will enable these poor families to come out of their poverty at least in the next generation. I can assure our political leaders that the *aam aadmi* or the poor, having realised the value of education would prefer this alternative any day to the kerosene subsidy or other doles.

The Railways have been bleeding for the last 10 years under ministers ostensibly working for the *aam aadmi!* Therefore, the courageous and long overdue step of an across the board increase in railway fares announced on 9th January should be strongly applauded. Instead, the tariff increases were instantly criticised by the BJP and CPM as being anti *aad aadmi* and anti-poor. This is so disingenuous and dishonest. The fact is that the fare increase will help Railways to stop making losses, enable it expand its network, undertake necessary modernisation and improve facilities for ordinary passengers. These activities will generate employment and also provide much needed connectivity for the poor people living in remote areas who have no other means to escape from their miserable local environment and search for jobs and better living conditions in other parts of the country. The increase in the Railways fares is clearly pro *aam aadmi*.

Similarly, household electricity tariffs are kept artificially low to protect the *aam aadmi*. Consequently, state electricity boards (SEBs) are haemorrhaging and have accumulated a enormous loss of ₹261,264 crore between 2007-08 to 2011-12. This huge and persistent haemorrhaging precludes capacity expansion and does not allow even the critically needed upgrading of transmission and distribution networks. These results in long hours of power cuts that severely hamper industrial expansion and the related employment generation. The adverse impact is only on the poor as the well-off get away with their inverters and generating sets. So it will be far better if SEBs earned a surplus, which could be used for capacity expansion and reducing crippling electricity shortages. That would help the poor far more. It is instructive to note that per capita availability of electricity in India is a mere 778 Kwh, one-fifth of 3428 Kwh in China and less than one-twelfth of 12000 Kwh in the US. Raising electricity tariffs will help the *aam aadmi*.

Finally, fertiliser subsidies, amounting to a whopping ₹67,198 crore in 2011-12 are supposed to help the *aam aadmi!* It is well established that this huge subsidy almost entirely benefits either the fertiliser companies or the middle and large farmer who are its major users. The rural *aam aadmi*, the marginal farmer and the landless labourer cannot and does not benefit from this subsidy. Instead this vast amount of public expenditure could have been used for expanding public irrigation systems, improving ground water availability and building rural roads and other infrastructure. No one with any honesty can argue that removing the fertiliser subsidy and re-directing it to other uses as pointed out above will not be more beneficial for the *aam aadmi*.

The list of such mis-directed and ill-conceived policy measures can be further amplified. The dishonesty of the claim that these help the common women or man is sickeningly clear. Yet the entire political class and senior bureaucracy persists with these measures and the attendant hypocrisy. One wonders at the real motivation, which drives the policy makers of all political hues in to doing this.

These populist policies have an even more harmful consequence. They are creating a culture of entitlements from which it will become increasingly difficult to wean away the non-poor beneficiaries. This entitlement culture breeds corruption, inertia and dishonesty. Instead we could use the same amount of resources to train people, educate them, improve access to quality health services, reduce power cuts, make them better connected and in overall terms make the *aam aadmi* more empowered. In a poor country like ours, empowering the *aam aadmi* and increasing their productivity is far superior to addicting them to leaky entitlements.

41

Global Dimensions of Anna Hazare's Movement

I WONDER IF those who see a foreign influence on Anna Hazare's movement realise how close they are to the truth. As I argue below, global trends now unfolding have a major influence on our social and political realities. Not of course in terms of the rather silly charges of conspiracy and the hidden hand but in deeper more structural manner. Hazare's movement, aided and abetted unwittingly by the ruling establishment, has pushed all other burning issues to the background and now threatens to wipe out the monsoon session of the Parliament. This is indeed a great pity as we were earnestly hoping that the session would be used for pushing forward the slew of important legislations which have been hanging since long. This is the only method to reverse the perception of policy drift and help get the economy back on the high growth path. Perhaps it is time for the industry, whose interests will be vitally affected by the likely social and political turmoil that would ensue if the current impasse persists, to try and get the two sides to converge. Let us not forget that the real cost of political turmoil are ultimately borne by the people who lose livelihoods and incomes. The industry with its focus on possible loss of global competitiveness due to avoidable uncertainty and loss of production has a direct interest in ending the stand-off.

India should at this time be making extra efforts to ensure that its domestic investment climate remains attractive, its institutions are seen as robust and accountable and social and political stability is maintained. Those amongst us who have delusions of creating a Tahrir Square in Delhi are doing the nation grievous disservice. The global economic and political situation is almost teetering on turning ominous. Stock markets all over the world, including ours, are reflecting this extreme nervousness about short term prospects both in Europe and the US. These two economies, which account for nearly half of the global output, are spluttering and in real danger of grinding to a halt. I am told that nearly a quarter of the young population in major European countries is presently under or unemployed and in the US the long term structural unemployment is also close to a fifth of the working population. These are frightening numbers in countries which are no more used to such sharp divides within their populations. Europe with its under capitalised banks, stubborn fiscal deficits, rising public debts, ageing populations, slowing growth and political divisions that are becoming sharper, is virtually on the edge of a calamitous precipice. The US recovery has pretty much ground to a halt and the expenditure cuts forced by the belligerent right wing of the Republican party will not help matters. Housing prices remain stuck at their lowest since the Lehman crisis and fears of a double dip recession are now more widespread than ever before. The worst prognostications made by the indefatigable Paul Kruegman seem to be coming true. Not only are his recommendations for greater public expenditure ignored, the Tea Party stalwarts are forcing cuts when they will hurt the most. The downgrading of US debt, stagnant consumer spending, persistent unemployment, and massive slowdown in corporate investment have stymied all prospects of a quick and robust US recovery. All this does not bode well for the US economic prospects which may get worse before they get any better. With the trans-Atlantic economies barely keeping their heads above water, the centre of gravity of the global economic activity, investors' attention and job seekers searches will inexorably shift eastwards to Asia including South Asia and India.

All these global trends are directly and strongly related to Anna Hazare's movement. With dimming economic prospects in the West, investors are looking with greater interest and serious intent at investment prospects in emerging economies like India. This greater interest by foreign investors translates in to demands for and greater pressure on achieving more transparency in rules and procedures that affect investment. We are just beginning to realise the higher governance requirements of attracting greater volumes of FDI in to the country. Secondly, and more importantly, with the US and Europe not attractive any longer, the Indian elite does not have the escape route which took them away from the corrupt and dysfunctional procedure ridden governance systems in the country. Now that they have nowhere to go, they have finally focused on the need to set things right at home. Better late than never, and this bodes well for us. Thirdly, the Indian industry, having expanded, globalised and hence more exposed to best practices during the past two decades since liberalisation speaks more freely and cogently against corruption and crony behaviour which puts the large majority of them, the honest and hard working entrepreneurs at a distinct disadvantage. Finally, the global explosion in information and social networking has taken firm roots and blossomed in India. Facebook and Twitter and the internet are all global phenomenon that have been successfully 'Indianised.' The middle class now has unprecedented means to express its frustrations and mobilise public opinion around them. All these four factors, directly and intimately linked to the global phenomenon, have strengthened and reinforced Anna Hazare's movement. The issues he has raised, endemic as they are, will have to be addressed by passing a robust Lokpal Bill and by taking several other necessary measures.

42

No Magic Formula for Gujarat's Achievements

GUJRAT with 5 per cent of the country's population contributes 16 per cent of India's industrial output and more than 22 per cent of its exports. Its agriculture rate of growth on an average has been around 10 per cent, when the national average is 3 per cent. It has reversed the trend in groundwater depletion and provides 24x7 supply of electricity to rural households.* And surprise surprise, farmers pay for the electricity consumed!**

It is somewhat disingenuous to argue that Gujarat has done well now simply because Gujarat has always done well. Punjab once had the highest per capita income in the country but is now faced with industrial decline, agriculture stagnation, looming water groundwater crisis, and sharply rising incidence of drug and alcohol addiction among the youth. West Bengal, the most industrialised and progressive state at one time, regressed during the three decades of CPM misrule. Thus, initial conditions and inherent potential do not mechanically determine outcomes. Effective policy intervention and leadership is necessary for converting them into positive outcomes.

There is no magic formula for Gujarat's achievements. Mr Modi's economic success has been based on a time tested and amazingly simple model. There are two principal components of this model. First, creating conducive business climate (captured fully in Modi's mantra of red carpet not red tape for investors) to attract increasing volumes of private investment to fuel rapid growth. Second, to sustain the growth momentum by honest and effective governance that ensures effective delivery of good quality public goods and services for the

---

*: See Stockholm Water Institute, *World Water Week, Report* No 31, 2012, p.22.

**: See : Revision of Tariff Effective from 1st April 2013, Circular from Madhya Gujarat Vij Private Ltd., dated 26 April 2013. *http://www.mgvcl.com/Tariff_01_04_2013.pdf*, p.2 and 8.

all the people. The government is seen to be committed to provide equality of opportunity for all without any discrimination. In essence, this model has investors and government working together for economic advancement with the government ensuring that benefits of growth are evenly spread and inequalities are not exacerbated. One of the consequences of this approach is to eliminate the spurious trade-off between growth and equity—both can and must be achieved simultaneously to sustain growth.

Another consequence of Modi's approach will be greater emphasis on implementing the 'right policies' rather than to either be only rhetorical about what needs to be done or to go in search for silver bullets or out of the box solutions. Gujarat has shown that the key to success is to focus on implementation of well-known policies required to make the transition out of a low income economy. There are several examples of this focus on implementation. The single window system for new investors; the breakthrough achieved in river connectivity and canal extension; the use of drip and sprinkler irrigation system for water conservation; augmenting groundwater resources; organisation of Krishi Mahotsava for exposing Gujarat farmers to advances in agrarian practices and technologies; sending more than a lakh of government workers for contacting farmers in an attempt to resuscitate agro-extension services; completing river basin development programmes for rain water harvesting etc. etc. Modi has shown that effective, time bound implementation of projects and programmes which have been designed after due diligence and consultations is the key to good economic performance.

It is not clear that Mr Modi will be able to deliver a business friendly policy framework in Delhi because of coalition compulsions. His Gujarat experience may not be entirely relevant in tackling the macro challenges which State governments are not concerned with. Given the much larger policy canvas, he will have to set himself clear priorities to avoid spreading himself too thinly. A different approach will be required to connect with investors when the central government has little control over ground realities, which are controlled by State governments. But the focus on implementation can be transferred with good effect and this may well be his single most important comparative advantage. He must start preparing now to successfully make the transition from a provincial setting to the national and global scene.

There is some criticism that human development indices in Gujarat have not improved as much as in other states, despite the undeniable strong growth performance. What is surely now required is a round of aggressive positive discrimination to ensure universal access to good quality education and primary health especially for the lower income groups. This will provide even greater sustainability to Gujarat's successful development model. It will also be important to focus greater attention to improvement in human development indices by adopting a more dynamic approach to poverty reduction that constantly focuses on improving the welfare of the last income decile of the population.

43

Lessons from the Semi-Final

THE MOST IMPORTANT LESSON from the elections in the four major states is loud and clear. It is not going to be business as usual in Indian politics. This may well be the watershed in the development of Indian democracy and India reaching its 'progressive moment' when the old world politics with its features of casteism, money power, muscle power, hereditary privileges and rank opportunism gives way to the new issue based politics that derives its electoral appeal from being based on grass root movement, accountability of the party in power and a strong anti-corruption and good governance platform. Such a conclusion is due not only because of the amazing debut of the Aam Aadmi Party (AAP) but also because of the third term won by both Shivraj Singh and Raman Singh. And the resounding defeat of Ashok Gehlot who spread government largess in the last one year as if there is no tomorrow. The defeat of Sheila Dikshit, a front runner in the polls for her personal capability must show to the Congress 'high command' that what they or their minions do in the name of the party sticks to people's memories which are no longer as short as some of the Congress power brokers like Ahmed Patel and Janardhan Diwedi (the two who accompanied Sonia Gandi to the press conference where she accepted defeat) would have us believe.

The hypocritical 'pro-poor' stance of the Congress party which combines its charity at public cost with feudal and ultra-elite living style has been shown to be what it is—a complete sham and electorally defunct. The voters from Delhi, with its high middle class population and from Chhattisgarh with its high share of tribal population which is excluded, have demonstrated that this is now a country of a billion aspiring people who want good governance to achieve rapid and sustained growth. They will accept the handouts either of 'public subsidies' or the bottle of booze on pre-election night, but will vote for those who will be seen as representatives and not the rulers and whose credentials for honest and efficient delivery of public services are relatively better. They will not be hoodwinked any longer by charity and handouts from those who hide in sheer luxury behind high walls, 'enjoy most heavy partying into the night' only to then publicly hold forth in a perpetually angry voice on behalf of the excluded.

We cannot go overboard and begin to believe that from now our democracy, which has certainly passed a historical milestone today and demonstrated in great measure the wisdom and sagacity of the Indian electorate, is on auto-pilot. There is a long way to go before all those who win elections exclusively on the basis of identity and dividing the community or with the help of '*bahubalis*' or by throwing goodies at the people are thrown irretrievably in the dustbin of history. To achieve that the necessary condition is the rapid growth of the middle class which in turn is based directly on rapid economic growth and spread of modern industry and technology. These elections as those earlier in Karnataka have demonstrated that the division between the rural and urban voters and more generally between 'Bharat' and India is increasingly irrelevant. Indians are now being driven by the universal urge to improve their material existence and ensure that the next generation lives better than them. To push this movement further forward the media, civil society and the Indian intellectuals will have to work with even greater honesty and drive and not relent. The Bharatiya Janta Party (BJP) for example must realise that it is not their promise of 30 per cent cheaper electricity or the promise to give 12 instead of 9 gas cylinders that have allowed them to scrape through on this occasion. The clean image of Harshvardhan, the modern working style of Nitin Gadkari and perhaps above all the dynamism and openness of Narendara Modi who addressed more rallies in Delhi than all other national BJP leaders taken together, were responsible for getting them barely past the post. I can bet that if the party had not declared Harshvardhan as their chief minister candidate, the Delhi electorate would not have hesitated to dump them along with the Congress. Even now they will have to be on their toes with a strong opposition led by a person who has national aspirations based on pushing ahead with the anti-corruption and good governance agenda. Perhaps Delhites will get a government that is not a ruler but a service provider as the BJP campaign posters have promised.

Since the exit polls made it clear that Congress will be routed and today as that rout became a reality, some journalists and all the spin doctors of the Congress have gone out of the way to assert that the outcome of these four state elections has no bearing on the forthcoming general elections. This is sheer living in denial. Thankfully, the president and vice-president of the Congress did not repeat this and admitted to the need of a deep introspection at this stage. This introspection should not lead them in the wrong direction of denying the present challenge and escaping in to the mirage of organisational restructuring, which as we know happens best when the organisation is grappling with the problem at hand rather than in classroom lectures and on the drawing boards of well meaning consultants. Mahatma Gandhi did not hold leader training workshops with elegant graphics to make the Congress a deeply democratic and dynamic force. Yes, the material and technological conditions may have changed but the means of motivating the cadre remains pretty much unchanged. It will be advisable to learn from AAP's thumping debut and Kejriwal's success rather than from foreign consultants. For that the Congress vice president will have to immerse fulltime into politics, warts and all, and not do it on the weekends for selected photo-ops.

For the BJP, it is time for even greater effort. Vasundhara Raje has demonstrated how sustained hard work pays off handsomely. Modi has led from the front on this. But they can now slip into complacency. That would be fatal. AAP's leaders surely realise that the rest of India is not Delhi. Communicating their message to raise an army of millions of volunteers and not thousands that sufficed for Delhi will be tough when the internet penetration is only 12 per cent and social media still largely an urban phenomenon. With their arrival, however, there is a prospect that elections will once again become a festival of democracy and not the dreadful and deadening dirge of cynical professionals who used elections for illegal gratification and couldn't give a damn about the people. We can all be optimists again.

44

BJP: Time for its Own Vision

2013 HAS DELIVERED from its throes of economic downturn and despair a brand new political party. Aam Aadmi Party's (AAP) emergence is perhaps the most disruptive event in India's post independence political history. By forming the government in Delhi AAP has queered the pitch for the BJP who expected to benefit from people's anger against the Congress to win the forthcoming Lok Sabha elections quite easily. With the Congress Party virtually accepting defeat and Rahul Gandhi already focusing on the 2019 elections, BJP and Narendra Modi would do well to shift focus from Congress to working out a viable strategy to meet the challenge posed by a rapidly emerging AAP. BJP will do well to keep in mind that in 1977, Janta Party was cobbled together in a mere three weeks and went on to rout Indira's Congress. BJP has to effectively counter this growing electorate infatuation with AAP.

BJP should not assume that AAP's appeal cannot and will not spread beyond the middle class dominated Delhi. This is to deny the power that the electronic media now has in forming voter perceptions even in the remotest corners of India and in blurring the distinction between rural and urban voters as far as messaging and opinion making is concerned. The image of an AAP minister visiting the night shelter at midnight and the news of power tariffs being reduced by 50 per cent will travel in micro-minutes across the length and breadth of the country and leave deep impressions on the voters' minds. Therefore, BJP has to proactively occupy centre stage in the national media. BJP would do well to realise that the reach of the media is manifold larger than any mega rally it can organise for its prime ministerial candidate. BJP cannot secure a strong presence in the media simply by depending on its motley group of spokespersons who work without a consistent script and are unable to inspire the viewers.

Today BJP needs a 'book of ideas' which will allow the spokespersons to speak in a cogent, forward looking manner and not simply react to emerging situations almost in an 'off the cuff' manner.

BJP has to quickly change its current twin strategy of Congress-bashing and showcasing Gujarat's success. The former is now becoming a bit redundant as even astute observers like Vinod Mehta do not give Congress more than double digit number of seats in the next Lok Sabha. So to mock the prince and his entourage will yield only diminishing returns here on. To go beyond Gujarat, the BJP led by Narendra Modi has to demonstrate that as in Gujarat, it has a vision for the country which will inspire the voters, especially the young ones, and attract them to the Party. This was done successfully in all the three states where the Party was victorious in the recently concluded state elections. Such a vision if properly articulated can prove to be the much needed 'book of ideas and issues' which the party has lacked so far and from which its cadre and spokespersons can offer an development agenda for the electorate. It will also allow the party to make a far better impression on the national media, thereby influencing views and opinions across the country. The national media has already started to demand that BJP's prime ministerial candidate spells out his ideas of how he sees India's evolution in the coming years. This demand will only become stronger. This demand will be met effectively by producing an inspiring well articulated vision that would also influence and dominate public discourse during the run up to the elections.

BJP could enhance its credentials for participative democracy by putting forward its vision document as a public document for wider public discussion. This will surely energise the campaign beyond rhetoric and skillful public oratory and reduce the distance between the BJP political brass and the common voter. This distance is unfortunately seen to be as large as in the case of security obsessed Congress leadership. By publicly discussing the vision draft, BJP will have a better chance to re-occupy the mind space that it has surely ceded to AAP with its 17 point agenda, which it hammers away with great effect.

Today the people demand not mere generalities, vague assurances and promises but more specific plans and measures. BJP's vision will therefore have to be backed up with detailed targets and timelines with corresponding policy measures to show that the party has a solid grasp of the issues and is intellectually equipped to take the country forward. To shy away from targets and timelines will allow AAP to completely takeover the policy space for inclusive growth. People today expect political parties to not only spell out their programme but also demonstrate their will and capacity to implement it.

BJP should unequivocally make the case for a market-based, private sector led sustainable and inclusive growth. It is important for it to publicly state its understanding of how an efficiently regulated private sector, when working together with an effective and efficient government can deliver the highest rates of inclusive and sustained growth. This will highlight the contrast with AAP, whose populist and statist policy prescriptions can result in a reversal of the reform process, which will be disastrous for the country. For example, it would not at all be surprising if after a Comptroller and Auditor General (CAG) audit of Discoms, AAP moves to re-nationalise electricity distribution in Delhi to implement its policy of subsidised electricity to its middle class supporters. This would be an unmitigated disaster.

It will be far better for the BJP to state its position on the entire range of issues clearly and cogently as it will then present a viable alternative to that presented by the Congress and more importantly by AAP. To not take up this intellectual challenge has a high risk of the party losing credibility with the electorate and its prime ministerial candidate being seen as an expert communicator but who does not have a solid, coherent well thought plan of action for the country. And its spokespersons and Lok Sabha candidates will be constantly reacting or making promises that may be seen to be inconsistent with national interest. This would indeed be a pity because Mr Modi at present has the credentials for being both an efficient administrator and one who has a vision for the country. But as yet the electorate is not sure of the direction in which he will take the country. It is, therefore, time that he publicly articulates this vision and puts it out for deeper and wider scrutiny.

IV

South Asia

45

Reimagining South Asia

THE ECONOMIC CASE for a regionally integrated South Asia has been demonstrated beyond any conceivable argument against it. The region will benefit in multiple ways if borders that today divide countries would become porous and permit a free exchange of goods, services and movement of people. Major issues like the harnessing of the region's massive hydropower resources, addressing the growing concerns about climate change and environment, and tackling cross-border human and drug trafficking can only be tackled if the South Asian countries work together and cooperate with each other. Some progress has of course been made, most importantly in India's expressed willingness to assume asymmetric responsibilities for pushing forward the agenda of regional cooperation. Despite these advances, a visitor to the region could not but get the feeling that the underlying sentiment or the idiom of discourse and dialogue in the region is still the 1947 mindset in which competition predominates over cooperation; mistrust effectively erodes confidence building measures; security concerns are always allowed to trump mutual desire for greater commerce and a bellicose media is permitted to fuel xenophobic and parochial emotions. Is this hugely unsatisfactory status quo destined to remain unchanged during our lifetime?

Some of us in all South Asian countries are committed to work towards changing this unsatisfactory state of affairs. On them falls the onus for making an intellectual case for regional integration (not simply regional cooperation) that is strong enough and is disseminated widely enough to fire the imagination of the people of this region in support of regional integration. We have to show beyond doubt that regional integration is a positive sum game and in fact lack of cooperation could land us in serious trouble with our young populations being sucked into interminable rounds of hostility and conflict. That will be a costly waste of the demographic advantage that South Asia currently enjoys.

After working for nearly 30 years on South Asian regional cooperation, it is now clear to me as never before that the onus for pushing this agenda forward falls on us in India. In some ways this is only natural as India's economy, population, geographic area, the size of its armed forces, the number of billionaire industrialists, is larger than the combined total of all other countries in South Asia. It is the only country in the region with land borders with more than one country and its population comprises all religions, ethnicities and cultural groups found in any of its neighbouring countries. Therefore, what happens in India and whatever India does is watched with a hawk's eye in all the other South Asian capitals as it directly and often significantly determines the turn of events in these countries. Therefore, India must recognise and accept this responsibility for ensuring the region's stability, prosperity and integrity.

Seen in this context, it will be surely difficult to argue that India does not or cannot influence the domestic situation in neighbouring countries. To argue on these lines is to abandon our claims to be a regional power let alone aspire for a global role. Having recognised its legitimate role in the region's affairs, India has to do whatever it can to prevent the spread of *Jihadi* ideology and influence both in Pakistan and Bangladesh. Similarly, the rise of Sinhala/Buddhist extremism in Sri Lanka or the lack of progress in the restoration of full human rights and equality of opportunity for Jaffna Tamil population require an active policy stance on our part to influence the outcomes. India has to prevent any further strengthening of the extreme radical fringe of Maoists in Nepal in the interests of both the Nepalese people and in the interest of its own internal security. It will be in my view preferable to openly accept that India has active interests in the neighbourhood and for which it will try to influence the emergence of positive outcomes, in close consultations and collaboration with concerned governments. To deny such interests in our neighbouring countries and yet pursue them covertly reduces our degree of freedom and also creates an environment of mistrust as practice on the ground does not conform to the rhetoric of having a 'hands-off' policy.

It is time that Indian political class shows the necessary understanding and courage and declare the promotion of South Asian Regional Cooperation as one of their priorities. Mr Nawaz Shariff made an improvement in Indo-Pakistan relations as an electoral issue and won a landslide victory. Improvement in bilateral relations with India could also be one of the main electoral planks for Sheikh Hasina in the forthcoming elections. Similarly, in Nepal several political formations openly declare their interest in developing better ties with India while going into electoral battle. It will therefore behove the Indian political establishment to reciprocate these sentiments and also reassure the neighbouring countries of their unwavering support in protecting their country's sovereignty, integrity and prosperity. Without such unambiguous and open support from the Indian political class, it will remain difficult to push forward the agenda for regional cooperation in South Asia. It is time that Indian political parties included successful regional cooperation in South Asia in their election manifestos and assign it the due priority.

The political class in India has to take a long term strategic view of South Asia and not let minor incidents on the borders or some extremist sentiments inside any of its neighbours deflect it from the path of achieving greater economic openness within the region. We have to go ahead with a more liberal and unilateral stance towards our neighbours offering them greater access to our domestic markets, welcoming them with a liberal visa regime and ensuring that our diplomats and other officials engage with them with sensitivity and with mutual self-respect. We should persist with these actions without expecting reciprocity, which will come when our neighbours are convinced that regional cooperation is positive sum game for all concerned.

46

Indo-Pak Trade Talks

Possible Breakthrough?

FROM ALL ACCOUNTS the recently concluded meeting between the Indian commerce secretary Rahul Khullar and his Pakistani counterpart has been exceptionally productive. Both sides have expressed their intent to explore the possibility of entering into a mutually agreed preferential trade agreement to further bilateral trade, extend tariff concessions on products of export interest to both countries and most surprisingly have also agreed to replace the positive list with a negative list. This is in line with South Asian Free Trade Area (SAFTA) and will open up a new era in bilateral economic relations between the two neighbours. Given my own interaction with a panel of other observers on a Lahore based television channel, I can say with some degree of confidence that we may well be witnessing a breakthrough in bilateral economic ties.

There are several reasons that justify a degree of optimism, even past history warns us against it. First, because for the first time ever perhaps the Pakistani side has mentioned as the granting of the Most Favoured Nation (MFN) status to India without linking it to any other condition. While the joint communiqué falls short of an agreement let alone a time line on this crucial issue, it does say that this will be a beneficial measure for both enhancing trade between the two countries.

Second, the meeting also discussed the opening up of second gate and new dedicated roads for passenger and freight traffic. This is a very significant decision which would have a positive long term effect in facilitating trade and commerce across the borders. At present, the movement of goods across the land border is restricted to only 150 trucks per day. With opening up of the second gate, there would be substantial increase in the movement of truck cargo. Third, at present, only 190 items are being allowed to be traded through the land route. It is heartening to note that Pakistani side would remove its present restrictions on trade by land route as soon as the required infrastructure is completed. This will surely result in a huge surge in trade. Fourth, both sides have also agreed to increase trading hours to take advantage of the new infrastructure, expedite clearance of cargo and facilitate movement of containerised traffic. Fifth, it has been agreed to include new products like petroleum products and BT cotton seeds. The export of BT cotton seeds to Pakistan from India will ensure better cotton yield and enhance the growth potential of the textile industry in Pakistan. And finally, both sides have also agreed to explore the feasibility of trading electricity.

All these measures, when implemented, would reduce transactions costs substantially as trade will be direct between the two countries rather than via Dubai or Europe as at present. The Federation of Indian Chambers of Commerce and Industry (FICCI), which has consistently supported a normalisation and expansion of economic ties between the two countries, strongly welcomes these developments and the decision to form working group which would not only address the issue of non-tariff barriers but would also resolve sector specific barriers to trade. Let us hope that the next step would be to jointly address the water issue which can only be resolved with the two sides working together and in good faith to address an issue that could soon reach critical status if not handled with sensitivity and a collaborative spirit. FICCI will as always be at the forefront in any effort for pushing forward with the economic integration of the South Asian space. The Indo-Pak trade talks could well mark a major milestone in this important journey.

47

Dealing with Different Pakistans

IN THE BROUHAHA OF Rahul Gandhi's most insensitive and mistimed remarks on the ordinance to overturn the Supreme Court ruling on disqualifying convicted persons from the Parliament, the meetings of our Prime Minister with his counterparts from Pakistan and Bangladesh received inadequate attention in the media. This is indeed a pity because for India, its neighbourhood in South Asia (extending from Kabul to Yangon) is and will remain of critical importance. It is naïve to believe that India can achieve its development goals or its global ambitions if its neighbourhood is plagued with rising social instability, possible political implosion and rising economic distress. India has to proactively ensure that peace and prosperity reigns in South Asia.

The meeting with Sheikh Hasina, India's firm and openly declared ally, would have surely gone over the issues of border enclaves and the sharing of Teesta river waters. How I wish that Dr Manmohan Singh was in a position to convey to her that the Indian political establishment had managed to reach to a consensus on the issue of water sharing as well as border enclaves, both of which, if settled, will surely improve the electoral prospects of Awami League. India needs to do whatever it feasibly can to ensure her victory in the next elections, which I am told may still elude her. Therefore, we need to achieve this consensus soonest and I hope the UPA will engage with the opposition parties to pass the necessary legislation in the next session of the Parliament and in time for the forthcoming elections in Bangladesh.To serve the national interest, BJP, must work closely with the government on this issue and ensure that the bill is passed in the beginning of the winter session of the Parliament.

The Teesta case demonstrates once again that Indian states now have a major influence on the conduct of India's foreign policy. This has been true for Tamil Nadu and Sri Lanka for decades. It is, therefore, time that we begin to conceive of institutional mechanisms to actively consult with our border states on issues concerning our neighbours. To this end, Centre for Policy Research (CPR) is launching an initiative to involve the stakeholders in our border states in an ongoing dialogue and engagement with their cross-border counterparts. We are hoping that this will allow us to focus on some micro and more granular issues that can be more easily resolved when the environment in the states is more supportive of cross-border cooperation.

Almost the entire attention in the media was focused on the Prime Minister's meeting with his Pakistani counterpart. Our Prime Minister and his team of advisors did well to push ahead with the meeting despite the high decibel campaign against it in the domestic electronic media. Is it not most intriguing that some channels like Times Now persists in anti-Pak hysteria and almost an xenophobic stance on India's relations with her Western neighbour. At the same time we have the same media house also supporting initiatives such as 'Aman Ki Asha', which purports to build goodwill between the two countries. A cynical surmise would be that such apparent inconsistency produces the best commercial outcomes and while TRPs for the TV channel remains high, the printed media continues to be viewed positively by the newspaper reading intelligentsia. There must be a self-imposed limit beyond which commercial interests must become subservient to national interests. In the absence of such self-regulation, regulatory intervention must surely be justified.

Given the undeniable power of the electronic media on swaying public opinion, it is important that our television anchors and panel warriors recognise, that we have to deal/engage with many different Pakistans at the same time. There is little gained and much to be lost to keep railing and fuming against the crimes of omissions and commission perpetrated by Pakistan!

Presently, there is no single, coherent and rationally driven Pakistani establishment with which India can engage with. In fact, there are clearly five different Pakistans viz., Islamabad, Rawalpindi, Lahore/Karachi, Peshawar, the wild lands of Wazirstan and the north-west frontier. These represent the civilian government, armed forces, business community, domestic religious establishment and the Jihadis. Each one of these has a varying perception of relations with India. To lose sight of this very wide differentiation in perception and degree of hostility towards India across these five different segments, is not merely stupid but downright dangerous. Only the armed forces and Jihadis are irrevocably opposed to improving Pakistan's relations with India. By not distinguishing between these five Pakistans, and painting all of them with the same black brush, we face the risk of all of them coming together to safeguard their country's sovereignty. This is exactly what the Jihadis and the armed forces desire. By not distinguishing between these different constituencies, our TV anchors and so called hawks simply fall headlong into the trap of the Jihadis.

The practical implication of such a differentiated understanding of the situation in Pakistan is that we have to use both the carrot and stick simultaneously and persistently. Prime Minister Vajpayee did that admirably when he was bold enough to go out of his way to befriend Nawaz Sharif but then deal a crushing defeat on the Pakistani army in Kargil. Can our TV warriors not rise to the occasion and adopt such a somewhat nuanced position? Can they not see that they play into the hands of the worst hawks in Pakistan by calling for retribution and breaking off all relations, whether cultural or on the sports fields, at every incident on the LOC? Instead, they should demand greater engagement between the civilian leaderships of the two countries, civil society representatives and business communities, who are all desirous of closer and more friendly bilateral relations. We should for example greatly simplify the visa regime and not treat all Pakistani visitors as potential spies or terrorists despite what our agencies will have us believe.

At the same time we must demand that the Indian government be resolute and unsparing in defeating the nefarious designs of the Pakistani army. We should support our government's effort to crush the Jihadis with the help, if required, from our global partners. I am sure we are capable of adopting such a differentiated approach towards our largest neighbour from whom we cannot simply walk away as others can do. A strong civilian government in Pakistan and a robust democracy is surely in India's interest. Our television channels should, therefore, ignore the TRPs and help advance the national agenda by taking a nuanced approach towards Indo-Pak relations. It is surely not too much to expect or is it?

48

Time to Be Bold

THE INDO-PAKISTAN bilateral economic and commercial relations were put on a firm path in September 2011 when the two commerce secretaries laid out a roadmap with specific milestones. This raised huge expectations. But Pakistan has been unable to meet its commitments as laid out in the communiqué. Of all things the nomenclature of granting the Most Favoured Nation (MFN) condition to India became a serious hurdle. There is now talk of the term being changed to 'non-discriminated country' to satisfy those who were not ready to accept the Urdu translation of MFN. I cannot see anyone guaranteeing that this version will go through because elements that can militate against importing much needed electricity from India, can surely still agitate to prevent Pakistan normalising its trading relations with us.

In the present circumstances, India should seriously consider giving unilateral access to its market for Pakistan and prune its negative list without waiting for the MFN status. India has a huge surplus in its formal bilateral trade with Pakistan. This widens further in India's favour when the Dubai trade is taken into account. India's unilateral granting of better market access will thus not materially harm India's interests. On the other hand, it could provide a real fillip to Pakistani exports to India and thereby contribute to improving its economic performance. Perhaps equally importantly, the unilateral gesture by India will provide major ammunition to those stakeholders in Pakistan who support better ties with India. This unilateral measure will generate broad-based goodwill for India that will contribute to weakening the Jihadi's case against India. Clearly, India's security interests, of which political stability within Pakistan and weakening of the Jihadi support base are two principle components, will be directly served by this measure.

The case of the Turkmenistan-Afghanistan-Pakistan-India (TAPI) gas pipeline is an instructive one for understanding the convergence between India's national security interests and improving economic ties with Pakistan. TAPI was proposed initially proposed by the ADB in 2000-01. The other three countries moved with alacrity and set up a formal mechanism to push forward with the ambitious project. India on the other hand rejected it on security grounds. It took more than 10 years for India to finally see the merit of joining TAPI, which has been confirmed just yesterday by the new petroleum minister Mr Moily. TAPI, when completed and on-stream, will generate more than $500 million of 'wheeling charges' for Afghanistan. These will come mostly from India and will only reinforce India's already good relations with Afghanistan. This will directly serve India's security and political interests. The pipeline which will also deliver much needed gas to Pakistan and India at cheaper rates will create a mutual dependence in the safeguarding of the pipeline. Yet India's MEA (Ministry of External Affairs) establishment, for an inordinately long time and despite the championing of the project by the line ministry, took a narrow and short-term view of India's security interests and let the project drag on for more than 10 years. This mindset has to change. India has to take a more strategic view of its security interests.

For India, it is now important to build trust-based relationships with its neighbours, given that China is now actively trying to create a dominant presence in the South Asian economic and geographic space. Regional cooperation, mediated by external agencies like multilateral development banks would help build trust-based relationship in South Asia. It will be far better placed to counter the growing Chinese influence if its neighbours developed vested interests in the larger South Asian economic space. Therefore, India will have to further intensify its asymmetric approach towards its neighbours, which began in 2007, and take the responsibility for creating a more trust-based relationships with them.

India can take two other major steps to build greater trust with its neighbours. First, it should give national treatment across its territory for all freight movement from South Asian countries including

Myanmar. This would dramatically reduce shipment time and costs and enable South Asian countries to exploit the huge advantage of proximity. This one step by India will go a long way in reversing the geographic fragmentation of South Asia that came about in 1947. This suggestion has been made strongly by Mr Shyam Saran himself, who is currently the Chairman of the National Security Advisory Board. Second, it is time that India adopts a far simpler and liberal visa regime for its neighbours. The anachronistic and dysfunctional visa regime between Pakistan and India that is a major deterrent to commerce and tourism needs to be changed immediately. Visa regime with Bangladesh has already been substantially liberalised and the process should continue until the system for visa on arrival for all SAARC members is put in place.

Both these suggestions will be expectedly opposed by Indian 'agencies' on security grounds. This opposition reflects inertia in modernising our security apparatus and is based on the spurious logic that India, which is one of the six countries in the world with advanced missile technology cannot ensure its security except by adopting the most primitive measures like requiring its visitors to report to the nearest police station within 24 hours of their arrival.

In short the argument is that for India, to take an even more proactive and asymmetric approach towards its neighbours is in its long term strategic interests. Therefore, unilateral actions *vis-á-vis* its neighbours, especially Pakistan, which is the second largest economy in South Asia, as suggested above, should be seen to be in India's strategic interests and as safeguarding its security. These are not acts of magnanimity or generosity. Moreover, India cannot aspire to be a global player if it cannot ensure stability, peace and prosperity in its neighbourhood. Improving bilateral economic and commercial relations with Pakistan must be an important component of this strategy.

49

India-Pakistan Relations

Why We Have to Be Pro-active

I HAVE BEEN GRATIFIED by the unexpectedly large response to my previous column on future prospects of Indo-Pak commercial relations. Not all of it has been supportive of my optimism about these prospects. Quite clearly there is interest but also misperception and lack of adequate understanding of India's options in this strategically important relationship. Hence this sequel.

The response I received can be put in three categories. First, that the red-carpet treatment given to the visiting Pakistan Commerce Minister and my own rather over enthusiastic view of future possibilities reflect a north Indian fixation with Pakistan. These readers argue that Indo-Pakistan relations are not a priority for entire India. Look at Pakistan from the south of the Vindhyas and priorities and options would look very different. For that matter even our relations with China are perceived differently from the Deccan and Nilgiris. From a 'Southern Indian' view, the best course would be leave Pakistan well alone and let it stew in its own juices. Benign neglect would be the best policy option.

The second set of readers wanted me take a more balanced view of future prospects in light of the track record of bilateral relations. These are marked by rising bonhomie for a period only to be brought crashing down by deliberate and cussed action on part of the malignant segment of the Pakistani establishment. This segment (read ISI), which does not want the relations to improve beyond a point, would rather have the kettle simmering and boiling over from time to time. These readers warned me that given ISI's implacable opposition to a real improvement in Indo-Pak ties, and the organisation's huge reach and influence in Pakistani society and statecraft, it is fruitless to pursue an agenda of greater cooperation between these two nuclear armed Siamese twins joined at the Rann of Kutch. The third set of responses not only mocked my optimism but wished and indeed felt sure about a coming implosion of Pakistan which according to them was already a failed state. A few, more confident of India's strategic prowesses, than they should be, wanted the Indian government to hasten the implosion as that would serve India's strategic interests.

The first and third set of arguments are relatively easy to handle. First, would the proposed Southern Indian attitude of neglect and ignore help India's own interests? I am afraid not. Issues such as optimal utilisation of west Himalayan rivers, increasing desertification in Rajasthan and Punjab, and lack of over-land access to West Asian and Central hydrocarbon resources and access to their markets for example cannot be resolved without working together with Pakistan. The benign neglect of Pakistan could surely result in a malignant spread of fundamentalism on both sides of the border. That will not help our cause. And an imploding Pakistan will send waves of refugees across the borders with fairly horrific consequences. This implosion will surely be accompanied by the establishment of a victorious Jihadi state in both NWFP (North-West Frontier Province) and the Punjab. This will resonate with Jihadi groups here in our midst and surely boost the ideology calling for all those espousing the establishment of the Pan Islamic state. And yes the Pakistani army will suffer a real blow to its credibility, legitimacy and pride, and will break up in its many ways but that will also imply the emergence of an independent fully armed hard-core Jihadi army which will see its only *raison d'etre* as spreading the movement further as fast as possible and at any cost. Does that sound like a better future for India?

The second response, which has the unfortunate history of the sub-continent on its side and sounds reasonable is effectively a call for inaction. It is more difficult to counter as historical evidence is in its favour. But to accept it and therefore stop trying completely is to accept that ISI is indeed all powerful and can effectively control the destiny of this region with its 1.5 billion people—99 per cent of whom do not share the ISI's view of their future. The Indian state and indeed the Indian business and its middle class cannot let down the entire South Asian people. Not for cause of charity or selfless behaviour.

But because our own destiny is tied inextricably to whether or not we can defeat the nefarious designs of a minute segment of South Asian society which in its utter cynicism and pursuit of very narrow self interest will stop at nothing. The only option therefore is to do whatever it takes to defeat the nefarious designs of this small coterie. The two-fold response to counter this 'low temperature war' by both covert and overt means is to one, make it increasingly expensive to launch operations designed to create chaos and enmity between the two people. And two, to do all we can to strengthen the business community and civil society in Pakistan. This will allow them to emerge as viable and robust counter-veiling forces to Rawalpindi. In present day operational terms this translates into unilaterally removing the non-tariff barriers against imports and investments from Pakistan, relaxing the visa regime for business travellers and hugely expanding the contacts between all segments of civil society. Let us remember that our national security will be achieved when we can influence the decisions in our neighbourhood and not simply by being reactive and defensive.

50

Calling Pakistan Army's Bluff

IN MY COLUMN (Dealing with Different Pakistans) I had argued that India will have to craft a differentiated strategy to deal with different groups in Pakistan. In this piece, I want to elaborate further on this as some readers questioned its viability. It is clear that there can be only one approach towards the Jihadis of all shades, which is to crush them to make it clear that in modern societies only the state has the monopoly of violence. India should also openly support the US and NATO on their drone attacks and everyone else who is fighting against Jihadis all over the world. It will be good domestically for our population to see India as reinforcing the global coalition against Jihad.

At the other end of the spectrum are the civil society and Pakistani business who are quite visibly sick and tired of the ongoing violence, fear the Talibanisation of Pakistani and have openly expressed and voted with their feet for better relations with India. They have done this despite being threatened with violence and death by the Jihadis. We must, therefore, reciprocate accordingly with boldness. There are two steps we can take without in any way jeopardising either our security or economic interests. First, we should immediately implement the liberal visa regime for all Pakistani visitors and do away with the shameful practice of giving restricted visas for a few cities. This is primitive and remains in force only and only because of the backwardness of our security agencies who persist with blanket security approach rather than be more technologically savvy and give the government more degrees of freedom in inter-state relations. Surely, modern technology can help track those who violate their visa conditions and surely too, Jihadis don't cross over with visas and through designated border check points. They come with covering fire in Keran.

Second, India should now seriously consider unilaterally liberalising its import regime rather than wait for Pakistan to grant it the Most Favoured Nation (MFN) status. Evidently, it is difficult for the Pakistan government, beleaguered as it is *vis-á-vis* the fundamentalist, to take this step. Also India already has a substantial trade surplus especially if we take into account Indian exports to Pakistan via Dubai and even London! By this unilateral liberalisation, as we have already done for other South Asian neighbours, we will improve the trade balance and more importantly will provide a huge leverage to Pakistani businessmen to raise a stronger voice for normalising ties with India. My sincere suggestion is for India to implement the protocol agreed between the two commerce secretaries without waiting for the MFN. My hunch is that it will become very shortly irrelevant with the growth in trade that will ensue in any case. On some occasions it is wise to forego the symbolism as it is quite often more form than substance.

To design India's possible approach to the civilian government in Islamabad, we will need to distinguish between the political class and bureaucracy and then categorise those who are close to the armed forces and others, which are relatively less so. In general I have noticed that the bureaucracy has far deeper and extensive ties with the armed forces. This could be for many reasons including that both come from the same professional family background and that the bureaucracy has had to be subservient to the army for decades. Very often Pakistani diplomats and bureaucrats appear to be liberal towards India but actually do only the army's bidding. So our better bet is to strengthen our relationship with that segment of the political class who openly profess their friendship towards India and are not Jihadi supporters. PML and MQM today qualify on this criteria and will be useful to develop ties between politicians of the two Punjabs and between Mumbai and Karachi. Frequent interaction should be organized between the legislators from the two sides, along with track two events involving politicians, business and academics from the two sides and meeting with the officials on the sidelines. These will help remove misunderstandings and build much needed trust between the politicians.

Vis-á-vis the Pakistan army, our stance must be uncompromising and punishing. Incidents on the line of control (LOC), covering fire for infiltration by Jihadis or suspected ISI involvement with Jihadi attacks as in Mumbai must invite immediate and disproportionate retaliation and retribution. Our government must give clear and unequivocal free hand to our armed forces to deal with the situation. This should include the dismantling of training camps across the LOC which really are a perpetual symbol of India's inability to shake off the nuclear bluff and allow Pakistan to persist with adventurism and continue with its policy of trying to bleed India with small cuts. It also allows the Pakistani army to continue with its coalition with the Jihadis who are given a free hand and support to attack India and take on Kabul and its allies as long as they do ISI's bidding. India will have to explain to the US, China, Russia and the NATO countries that these terrorist training camps are simply unacceptable as are ISI supported incidents. These incidents are also harmful for the Pakistani population because they allow the ISI and the army to determine nature of Indo-Pak relations and abort any promising opening.

Does this stance convert me to a hawk against Pakistan? No it does not. In fact I am sure that a large majority of Pakistanis want to have their army put in its proper place. It should stay in the barracks and give up grandiose ambitions that have cost Pakistan dear. For India it is stupid for our TV anchors and foreign policy hawks to ask for complete freeze on all contacts with Pakistan and breaking off all dialogue or interaction every time an incident happens on the LOC. This only serves the purpose of the Jihadis and Rawalpindi as it does not punish them but instead burns up the goodwill among the people that takes enormous effort and time to rebuild. The stick should be wielded on the culprits and not on friends. India has to help the peace loving people of Pakistan by throwing our full weight against their army and Jihadis and opening our markets, cricket fields, cultural platforms and hearts to the others, which are undoubtedly the great majority.

51

Historical Opportunity for Mr Sharif

DEMOCRACY is taking roots in our neighbourhood. Pakistan has successfully completed its first ever democratic transition with the previously elected government completing its full term. This is indeed momentous and we in India must do whatever we can to reinforce the process and extend to Pakistan all our moral and material support at this time. I have always argued that the most effective and sustainable means to reduce the role and stature of the armed forces in Pakistan is to strengthen other institutions. India would therefore directly serve its own interests by supporting the incoming government. We can and should pick up from where Mr Nawaz Sharif had left off before he was unconstitutionally removed by Musharaff, who has been shown his place in no uncertain terms by the electorate to be in the dustbin of Pakistan's history.

I have noted with some great satisfaction Mr Sharif's favourable remarks on improving ties with India and this being one of his top priorities. The news in one of the Indian newspapers that he gave precedence to Indian journalists over their Western counterparts is most welcome and I hope Indian leaders will do the same to journalists from our neighbouring countries. Such gestures go a long way. I am told that in his opening address to the newly elected National Assembly which will meet at the end of this month, Mr Sharif is likely to mention his objective of improving ties with India as one of the top priorities for his government. All this is most welcome talk. But it has to be complemented with real action to take the agenda for improved Indo-Pakistani relations further. He has to take concrete steps to prove that the cynics in India who will have us believe that Pakistan cannot be trusted to keep its side of the bargain are wrong this time.

The first step must be to immediately grant the Most Favoured Nation (MFN) status to India. This was agreed by the previous government. I had accompanied Mr Anand Sharma in February 2012 on his visit to Lahore, Karachi and Islamabad during which we were told in no uncertain terms that the Cabinet had cleared the proposal and it would be implemented. Another year has passed and this has not happened. I am sure Mr Sharif realises that this has become one of those steps which must be taken to build Pakistan's credibility and its implementation will be far more than hundreds of long speeches in favour of building better ties between the two countries. I hope he will use his opening address to the Assembly to clarify to the Pakistani people that it is utterly dishonest to translate MFN as '*pasand deeda mulk*' and then use that for holding back its implementation. MFN only grants to India the same rights and privileges that Pakistan grants to all its trading partners. Mr Sharif will do well to clarify this to his constituents, announce its implementation and thereby take Indo-Pakistan relations to a qualitatively new level.

The joint statement issued at the end of the Seventh Round of talks between the Commerce Secretaries of the two countries (21 September 2012) clearly states that a number of further steps are linked to the implementation of the MFN. The agreement is that India will reduce its SAFTA sensitive list by 30 per cent after Pakistan has notified the removal of all restrictions on trade through the Wagah-Atari land route and reduce the sensitive list to a mere 100 items at six digit level once the MFN status has been granted (paragraph 12). The amazing goal of peak tariff rates of only 5 per cent on all items except a small list of 100 items on both sides before 2020 as agreed between the two commerce secretaries Mr S.K. Rao from India and Mr Munir Qureshi from Pakistan is surely attainable. The incoming prime minister will hopefully give it his fullest support.

May I suggest that Mr Sharif asks his commerce minister to prepare a timetable for the implementation of the agreements between the two commerce secretaries as expressed in the September 2012 joint statement. The Commerce Secretaries of the two countries, ably supported by their junior colleagues have done a commendable job in laying down a roadmap for improving the commercial relations across a wide range of sectors. It will be worth his while for Mr Sharif to spare a few minutes of his time to look at the Joint Statement and make its implementation a priority for his government. In doing so he will, I can assure him, be taking a historical step for South Asia.

The two countries have agreed to liberalise their visa regimes but this has also not been implemented. This needs Mr Sharif's immediate attention. Nothing is more effective in improving bilateral ties than greater people-to-people and business-to-business contacts. The new visa regime has to be put in place as soon as possible and then liberalised further. The fears of the Indian security agencies about misuse of the liberalised visa regime need to be addressed and this can be done simply by the new government accepting its responsibility in curbing cross border activities of Jehadi groups that are virulently opposed to further strengthening of Indo-Pakistan relations.

The re-coming of Mr Sharif already has historical significance. It is within his grasp to make it even more historical by taking the necessary steps to put Indo-Pakistan relations on a new trajectory and thereby bring prosperity and peace to the people of South Asia. Mr Sharif has in the past shown that he has the courage of his convictions to not let a small dangerous minority hijack the aspirations of the vast masses on both sides of the border. He has to take a few but critical steps now to prove his own credentials in this regard. Our best wishes and prayers are with him.

V

India and the Global Economy

52

India and Global Governance

INDIA IS NOW WELL and truly established as a member of the high table in the emerging global governance architecture. The process has taken about a decade, starting perhaps with the admission to the new quartet for informally steering the Doha Round in the World Trade Organisation (WTO), followed by becoming a member of the O-5 that was part of the Hellingendam-Aquila process and then being clinched by the membership of the G-20 and the related financial stability forum. With its coordinating role in some of the G-20 working groups and more recently the two year membership of the Security Council with the assurance from all but one of the permanent members of the United Nations Security Council (UNSC). This was done during the unprecedented six months of the latter half of 2010 when all the heads of government of all P5 States visited Delhi. Surely India had arrived as a global player and not confined any longer to a regional role.

It is important, however, to emphasise that a benign and indeed actively supportive external environment does not necessarily imply that India will also be an effective global player contributing to enhancing global welfare. This would require that Indian negotiators backed by the policy makers in Delhi are successful in reconciling the Indian national interests with 'global good' or are at least not perceived as recalcitrant players pursuing narrow and short-term agenda. This in turn requires that India is confident of the nature, trajectory and strength of its domestic economic growth. Successfully achieving rapid economic growth since the reforms in the early nineties and especially during the first decade of the present century has been the fundamental reason for the country to have found a place on the high table of global governance. India will have to sustain the rapid and equally importantly inclusive growth for the next three decades for it to credibly reaffirm its claim as a global player. I doubt if other global powers will give sufficient credence to Indian negotiating positions if the country's human development and social indicators remain at sub-Saharan levels. In short, India cannot take its nascent status as a major global player for granted. Its global status is derived from the global perception of the country's potential to emerge as the second or third largest economy in the world in the coming decades. This positive perception is already generating and has the possibility of generating far larger dividends from a benign external environment. However, it is not enough for the Indian economy to achieve 7-8 per cent rate of economic growth. With nearly 12 million new employment opportunities to be generated each year for the next 20 years and the explosion in individual aspirations, the Indian economy will have to expand at double digit growth rates. Moreover, this growth will have to be inclusive and environmentally sustainable. This is indeed a challenging objective but attainable. China was in a similar position in mid-eighties, a decade after it had initiated its own reforms under Deng. As we now know that China made fullest use of its opportunity and is now accepted as a global power. If, unlike China, India squanders this opportunity and the world community begins to perceive India as being unable to get its domestic policy act together, its global position will be quickly downgraded. Historical examples of Iran and then the Soviet Union should warn us in amply measures that such downgrades cannot be ruled out. Thus, there is simply no room for any complacency. India still faces many futures.

The four critical challenges or downside risks facing India in sustaining rapid and inclusive growth are its governance deficit, human resource development imperatives, infrastructure weaknesses and rising personal and regional income disparities. Rapid economic growth rate is the necessary condition for raising welfare levels. The sufficient condition is for the enhanced public revenues generated by higher growth to be used efficiently for removing poverty and implementing a comprehensive and efficient delivery of public goods and services. This requires good governance and an accountable system of public administration. Although India has strongly entrenched public institutions, its record since Independence in restraining corruption and mal-governance is substantially below par. This has meant a growing marginalisation of the poor in society and the sad spectacle of some human development indicators in India like child malnutrition being worse than Sub-Saharan Africa (SSA). This is simply neither acceptable nor sustainable. India will have to urgently improve the delivery of its social welfare programmes and direct cash transfers (when they are implemented next year) to ensure that higher rates of economic growth also yield greater inclusion and an improvement in the lives of the lowest deciles.

We also cannot take for granted the demographic dividend. It will have to be earned or it could well become a demographic nightmare if our large young population remains unemployed or worse still unemployable. Despite all that we may hear in the common media and perhaps contrary to external perception of India's education sector, the truth is that education capacities in the country have fallen dangerously behind demand. Only 12 per cent of Indian children find a position in the higher education system. The higher education enrolment in the US is above 80 per cent and in China it is reaching 20 per cent. While the enrolment in primary schools has reached 100 per cent, the quality of the education and curriculum is poor as reflected in several surveys conducted by civil society organisations. Vocational training is under developed with only 5,000 vocational training schools as compared to over 500,000 in China and a limited range of vocational courses on offer. The public education system is not in good health and the regulatory framework for quality assurance is archaic and under funded. India will have to take urgent and large scale reforms of its education system, including reducing the heavy burden of over regulation and liberalising the entry and role of private education providers at all levels to earn its demographic dividend.

The physical infrastructure deficit in India is now well established. It has emerged as perhaps the single most important constraint on the expansion of the manufacturing sector that is critical for generating the necessary employment. The Planning Commission estimates that nearly $ 1 trillion is needed in infrastructure investment during the coming Twelfth Five Year Plan (2012-2017). The main constraints on expanding infrastructure capacities appear to be, inefficient project implementation, archaic land acquisition laws, lack of coordination amongst various levels of governments and official agencies, relative paucity of public financial resources that is necessitating greater recourse to public-private partnerships (PPP) and measures to attract foreign capital in infrastructure sectors. The accumulated experience with PPP and finalisation of a robust regulatory framework will hopefully facilitate build up of infrastructure capacities in the coming years.

Rising inter-personal and regional income disparities could well get further exacerbated if growth is left entirely to the market forces as the more advanced regions within the country and better-off sections of the society will tend to benefit disproportionately. This increasing divergence across population segments is best reflected in the large wage differentials that exist between the organised labour segments which employ a mere 8-9 per cent of the total labour force and the unorganised sector where wages and productivity levels are much lower. Regional disparities are captured by catchy phrase, 'India *versus* Bharat', that is used to highlight the dualism that currently exists between advanced urban centres and the backward rural countryside that covers large parts of the country. These divergences or dualism if allowed to get exacerbated further could pose an existential threat to the integrity of the Indian nation state. The way forward, though not easy, is one to implement measures such as the universal Goods and Services Tax (GST), eliminate barriers against inter-state movement of goods and factors of production thereby creating a unified Indian domestic market, and to make labour laws more flexible so as to dilute the distinction between organised and unorganised labour markets. These measure require substantial political will and may not be easy in an era of coalitional politics. But there are some encouraging signs that state governments are beginning to see the benefits of such measures and could converge on some common set of policies. The set of four challenges and measures to address them will provide the necessary basis for sustaining rapid and inclusive growth in India during the coming decades.

It is clear that India will have to push forward on its reform agenda to sustain near double digit growth and generate sufficient employment for being able to play a meaningful global role. It is fruitless to debate over the primacy of a benign external environment or sustaining robust economic growth is a necessary pre-condition because the two are inter-linked. If priority has to be accorded between the two, we would do well to focus on implementing the domestic reform agenda and ensuring rapid and inclusive growth. Indian policy makers can safely assume that India's external environment will become increasingly benign as India sustains its rapid and inclusive economic growth.

Assuming that India is on the trajectory to successfully emerge as one of the three largest economies, it is useful to try and anticipate India's role and possible contribution to global governance architecture. This could be discussed in three somewhat distinct but closely inter-related aspects. First, in its regional neighbourhood, India will take on the responsibility for establishing a stable and prosperous South Asia. The importance of a prosperous South Asia for global stability and prosperity should not under-estimated. The region with more than two billion people in 2040 will account for nearly a fourth of the world population. An economically vibrant South Asia will be premised on a dynamic Indian economy and will imply the alleviation of poverty for nearly three quarters of the world's poor. India will continue with its newly found stance of accepting its asymmetric role and responsibility in the region. It will have to work hard and persistently to earn the trust and confidence of its smaller neighbours and ensure that the region remains peaceful and reverses the present trends towards religious fundamentalism and extremist left wing or ethnic violence.

Second, an economically resurgent India will necessarily be more globally integrated. Since the beginning of its reforms in 1991, 13 years after China started its reforms, the share of external sector transactions, including merchandise trade, two way services flows and remittances, has increased from about 20 per cent to nearly 60 per cent by 2009. This is likely to increase even more as India's domestic markets become more accessible for both imports and foreign direct and portfolio investment inflows through a series of free trade and comprehensive economic cooperation agreements. Furthermore, Indian firms, already foraying abroad in search of larger markets, primary resources and frontline technologies, will also invest in greater volumes abroad. India's economic interests will emerge as the primary driver of its foreign policy behaviour. This has two clear implications. One, that India can be expected to work together with other major powers in maintaining a stable and open economic order that is governed by universally accepted and multilaterally governed economic governance regime. Second, in the realm of global security and politics, it could be relied upon to join multilateral coalitions that aim to act against both existing and emerging overtly hegemonic powers or deviant leaders who do not play by the commonly agreed rules of the game. Thus, India will be drawn increasingly towards global efforts that are designed to establish universally accepted behavioural norms and seek to constrain unilateral behaviour for either achieving narrowly selfish national interests or avowedly in pursuit of some global objectives.

Third, given its past record and future stakes in a peaceful and stable global environment, India will also continue to support non-proliferation and actively advocate and work towards the 'zero option' of achieving a nuclear weapons free world. This is not mere rhetoric because Indians in general are not enamoured of overt destructive power. In addition, the concept of the entire globe comprising both the human society and nature, co-existing and thriving together is deeply ingrained in the Indian ethos. This ethos succinctly reflected in the sanskrit notation of '*Vasudhev kutukbum*' (the earth is one family) not only makes India a natural opponent of nuclear adventurism but more importantly also a inherent supporter of environment protection. The country's leadership will surely continue to oppose attempts to inequitably distribute the burden of environment protection, but its own people and firms have already initiated environment conservation measures that will surely intensify over time.

Finally, we can hope that India will become richer while not becoming less moral or humane in its social behaviour. If successful in this regard, and this is an even probability at present, India will be ranged along with countries fighting against women and narcotics trafficking. The optimism arises not from current dominant social behaviour that is unfortunately beginning to be dominated by rank materialism and conspicuous consumption but from the long tradition of moderation in all aspects of life. This will surely prevent India from being inextricably trapped in a materialistic and hedonistic morass which given the country's social complexity and dualist social structures could well be its undoing. Given its traditional wisdom and social heterogeneity, which acts as a constraint on any particular ideology or fashion, India will hopefully prevail over these downside risks and emerge as a democratic, ethnically pluralistic, economically prosperous and an ethical global player.

53

Need for Structural Reforms to Anchor the Economy amid Global Turmoil

THE GLOBAL ECONOMIC situation looks more fragile than ever. The present situation is perhaps worse than at the time of the Lehman crisis on several counts. Larger number of economies are involved; the crisis have been in the making for a while and represents a Tsunami that is overwhelming the defences that have been erected. The collateral damage, when the crisis is actually precipitated will be greater. And there seems to be practically no will for collective action as reflected in the near collapse of the G-20 dialogue at Cannes on global economic situation and the way forward. Unlike in the post Lehman period which saw purposive collective action at the Summit level, on this occasion everyone seems reconciled to pick up the pieces on their own and fend for themselves. With the US and France in full blown election mode and therefore focused entirely on domestic concerns; German leadership facing stiff domestic opposition against any large scale bail out and Japan in an ongoing somnolent policy stance, there is a frightening leadership vacuum at the global level. Among the emerging economies, China is too reticent, India relatively underweight and apparently lacking sufficient intellectual wherewithal and Brazil a bit unsure of its leadership material to fill this leadership vacuum. The International Monetary Fund (IMF) could have provided at least technical expertise but in any case it cannot substitute for the required political leadership. In such a situation one shudders to contemplate the consequences of another shock to the system in the form of the breakup of the Euro zone or a sharp sustained spike in commodity, including crude oil prices, as capital rushes to the relative safety of tangible assets and out of reserves held in fiat currencies. The non-acceptance of the German bonds by the markets on Wednesday, the 23rd of November shows that even the strongest sovereign offerings are seen as risky and in this scenario, appetite for fiat currency reserves could be very weak.

With the prevailing climate of each country fending for oneself, Indian policy makers in North Block, Udyog, Yojana and other Bhavans and on Mint Road have their task cut out. They must act urgently and in a coordinated manner to insulate the Indian economy from the coming Tsunami of exacerbated global turmoil. The policy objective can be summarised as restoring external and domestic investors' confidence in the economy by eliminating uncertainty. Additionally, efforts have to be made to achieving macroeconomic stability and implementing structural reforms for eliminating constraints on capacity expansion, which alone will help meet rising demands. In a word, policy makers need to take urgent steps to establish a 'Credible India' which can retain domestic capital and attract capital moving out of Europe and other advanced economies that are faced with investors' fatigue and rising turmoil. Having worked in the government, I realise that this is of course easier said than done. But a start must be made.

Fortunately such a start has been made by the Government's bold decision to allow 51 per cent FDI in multi-brand retail. The decision, apart from its benefits of attracting new investment, expanding employment, moderating the price of essential commodities and modernising the trade and agriculture sectors, will most importantly signal the end of policy drift and paralysis that had come to characterise the present situation. All those other measures that do not require legislative clearance and parliamentary approval should also be implemented right away. Another measure is to de-notify the perishables from the coverage of the APMC (Agricultural Produce Market Committee) act and allow the farmers to sell directly to any trader anywhere in the country. This will break the monopoly of a few registered operators in wholesale fruits and vegetable markets who act in concert to take advantage of any minor shortage and create inflationary spikes where none may be warranted. Here again there is apparent unanimity amongst all concerned, but executive action to be taken by state governments has been absent. The only exception perhaps is Bihar where the Act was de-notified during the first stint of Mr Nitish Kumar's government and has brought significant benefits to both the producers and traders by also helping to eliminate the rent-seeking behaviour of market inspectors and other petty bureaucracy. Finally the agenda of executive action must be the elimination of border taxes and octroi duties that act as avoidable barriers to inter-state trade and commerce. This should be accompanied with the removal of all barriers to cross-border trade for agriculture produce which results in waste in one location coexisting with scarcity in other parts of the country. As I have often said, India needs to sign a free trade agreement with itself prior to entering in to such agreements with other countries.

I have emphasised the agenda of executive action as it is doable and benefits arising from them have been well argued and documented. Actions detailed above will not only show the government's commitment to improving the business and investment climate but also bring real benefits in lower costs and prices. The agenda of reforms that require legislative action is also rather well known and principally includes reforms in the financial sector, tax regime and labour markets. Rather than repeat the list of these measures, I will like to focus on the need for all political parties to shed their partisan interests and act in the national interest at this critical time. This is not as difficult as it is made out to be. We have examples of such non-partisan behaviour by political parties at various times in our post independence history. The years 1962, 1965, 1971, 1991, 2000 are worth recalling when everyone came together for the national cause. Perhaps we have to work harder to convince our political class that the country faces real risk of being derailed from its path of rapid and inclusive growth. That is the task cut out for the readers of this column.

54

BRICS: India's Costly Timepass

THE FIFTH BRICS summit concluded in Durban, South Africa on Wednesday the 26th when most Indians were celebrating Holi, more mindful of water shortages in Mumbai than the creation of the BRICS Bank! The news about the bilateral meeting between our prime minister and the newly installed Chinese president Mr Xi Jinping grabbed more space and attention than the formation of the BRICS bank or the creation of CRA (Contingent Reserve Arrangement) with a corpus of $100 billion to assist members that face adverse market pressures against their currencies. I support the stand of the large majority of Indians to virtually ignore the BRICS process because BRICS is germane neither to India's over-riding domestic concerns nor indeed to its foreign policy objectives.

Prime Minister Manmohan Singh valiantly tried but in vain to infuse some purpose by enunciating a five point charter for collaborative effort. Quite expectedly, it was pitched at a high level of generality that made it rather inane. On the other hand, the existential problem faced by BRICS was spelled out by Vladimir Putin. With his tongue firmly in cheek, the Russian President likened the five to a grouping of Africa's big game trophy animals—the lion, leopard, elephant, buffalo and rhinoceros. All five strong in themselves, unable to accept another as leader and most importantly so widely diverse in their features that any coming together seems highly improbable. One wonders why then we have had five summits already?

In our book titled *In the National Interest: A Strategic Foreign Policy for India*, my co-author Santosh Kumar and I have argued for focusing our foreign policy on achieving and sustaining high rates of economic growth and generating more job opportunities. Having followed the BRICS (BRIC until 2011 when South Africa, a late entrant joined the grouping) process since its inception and having been present both at Sanya (2011) and Delhi (2012), I am not at all convinced that the BRICS process serves in any way this principal policy goal. What is the additionality or value added achieved in meeting together the heads of four countries over and above that accrue from timely and well prepared bilateral summits? Can the CRA actually come to our rescue if the Rupee comes under pressure as our current account deficit continues to widen and the credit rating agencies (god forbid) downgrade our standing to non-investment status? Would the highest policy attention of the PMO not be better and more effectively focused on ensuring that our exporters become more competitive and the foreign trade policy does not remain an annual ritual but instead gets a strategic focus that is backed by coordinated inter-ministerial action to provide better infrastructure and more conducive labour market conditions for Indian exporters to raise their dismal share in global export markets? I will be very surprised to hear any one argue that the BRICS process helps India to pursue its goal of rapid inclusive growth, which should be our exclusive policy concern for the time being.

It can be argued that it is unfair to evaluate the contribution of the BRICS process to our country's economic growth, critical as it may be. However, we must remember that India's aspirations of becoming a global power or a player are directly and strongly dependent on its economic performance.

One has to ask how the BRICS process serves the interests of India's external policy in an admittedly multipolar global community. The BRICS is seen by the rest of the world as an opportunistic assembly of five countries that have very few if anything in common between them. Other emerging economies question its legitimacy and argue for others like Indonesia, Turkey and Mexico being included and there is no valid argument against this except the existence of a clever acronym created by an American banker! Until recently a strong common feature among the BRICS was their rapidly growing economies. With the collapse of the growth momentum in Brazil, India and South Africa, this is no more the case. Any assumption of BRICS continuing to account for an increasing share of global growth is fraught with all kinds of downside risks. This becomes painfully true if one was to consider the BRICS economic performance excluding China. With such huge variations in their resource endowments, their current priorities, the dissimilarity of their macroeconomic conditions and much more so of their political dispensations, it will be miraculous if BRICS could sustain global interest in the summit process.

The real gainer from BRICS is clearly China. Prior to Sanya, the process was a desultory affair with hardly any serious attention given to it by the geo-strategic community. How many of us remember the town in which it was organized in Russia? (BTW the town was Yekaterinburg!) . As an emerged global power, China needs as many forums as it can have to display its rising prowess and show-off, especially to the Americans in the hope of converting its significant and growing economic clout into global political and strategic clout. I will be grateful to anyone who can explain how our participation in such multilateral forums serves the interest of either building a stronger bilateral relationship with China or to attract the attention of other emerging and developing economies to our own accomplishments in building a market based economy with a vibrant democracy combined with breath taking diversity.

The five countries have been unable to take even one meaningful tangible economic initiative since their inception. The much hyped BRICS Bank has expectedly emerged with a whimper as have so many previous such attempts at creating alternatives to the Bretton Woods twins. Extending the Putin analogy, the Indian elephant would do well to keep its eyes firmly on the ongoing dance of the eagle and the dragon and working to distance the two from each other.

55

Obama's Second Term Augurs Well for India

PRESIDENT OBAMA'S re-election was expected. We should remember that prior to the first Presidential debate, he had built a clear 10-point lead over Romney. This has now been re-affirmed by the clear victory that he has achieved. The tightness of the race during the last few weeks was in my view more a media creation and did not reflect the ground realities. At least the final tally with Obama winning 303 of the 509 electoral college votes and also winning the popular vote would tend to support this. I think people all over the world are heaving a sigh of relief because given the many changes in his stance on a wide range of issues, Romney would have been an unknown and I daresay an unpredictable entity to deal with. Whether we may agree with him or not, at least President Obama has the virtue of consistency in both his domestic and foreign policies. We can now be sure that the US will withdraw from Afghanistan, it will continue to press Pakistan to take a tougher stand against Islamic terrorists and not foment Taliban trouble across the Durand line. Let us hope that under his renewed mandate, the US will put sufficient pressure on the ISI (Inter-Service Intelligence) for them to realise that trying to calibrate the behaviour of the Taliban and expect its influence to remain confined on the other side of the border is a fools hope which they would do well to give up. With President Obama back in the White House, we can hope for an organised transition in Afghanistan in which India can play a very important and constructive role.

It is also a relief to realise that the US will now continue with its constructive engagement with China, putting mild but consistent pressure on China to conform to the rules of the game in global governance and in maintaining the multilateral trading order and strengthening the global financial architecture. Mr Romney had threatened to up the ante *vis-á-vis* China and that had the potential to create large scale dissonance in world markets and in the security sphere as well. With the new regime taking over in Beijing, a continuity in the White House and in the US stance towards China will be more comforting for those coming into power in China and encourage the liberal tendencies which can be expected to have greater political support with the ouster of Bo Xilai. President Obama's more sophisticated and nuanced approach towards maintaining US leadership position while continuously striving for broader coalitions and consensus is inherently superior to any 'Cold War like' stance in sustaining the present multipolar global order. G-20 may well get a new lease of life and even some new momentum with his re-election.

We have discussed the global and external implications for India of Obama's re-election not only because it is important that India's external environment remains stable and peaceful but also because unlike in the case of the Indo-US bilateral relationship, Delhi has very little role in shaping the contours of the global order. So it is helpful to realise that with Obama in the White House, India can expect another four years of relatively benign global environment in which it can pursue its development priorities.

The Indo-US bilateral relations will hopefully continue to further strengthen in the second term of Obama's presidency. The present Obama administration, pretty much across the board, has unambiguously shown that it wants to improve ties with India and raise them to the level of a working strategic partnership. In the last four years, the State Department has increasingly taken on India's concerns in its engagement in South Asia. The US expects India to play an important role in the newly launched Silk Road Initiative that attempts to bring Central and South Asia closer together. While being clearly disappointed, the US neither created too much of a fuss nor let the bilateral ties be affected when the large order for the next generation fighter aircraft went away to the French firm Dassault. And to the best of my knowledge the US has resisted the temptation to ask India to become a partner in any moves directed against China.

Over all the last four years have seen a consolidation of the Indo-US bilateral ties. With President Obama now being re-elected, there is clear possibility of not merely continued consolidation but to raise these ties to a higher level. If the Obama administration shows its willingness to raise the level of Indo-US engagement, it will be in our interest to reciprocate any such gestures. Perhaps the US will now insist on such reciprocity.

What could India's response be if the Obama administration in its second term offers a possibility of more intensive engagement? In my view, India will do well to continue with its mature and well honed policy response. This in effect has been to create a broad platform of diverse interactions between the two countries in attempt to achieve a steady, but certainly not a high velocity, deepening of the bilateral relations. Perhaps an additional element could be to ensure that we refrain from opposing the US on issues which may not necessarily impinge on our national interests. Moreover, India could try and emulate the French example of letting it be known to the US that while our broader interests converge sufficiently for us to become strategic partners, there will continue to be some differences in our stance towards global issues. The US will surely recognise and accept these differences as they are a result of our history, culture and compulsions of having to cope with the most heterogeneous, complex and diverse domestic polity.